Love and

MW01097953

A Guide To Family Healing

After the Loss of Your Baby

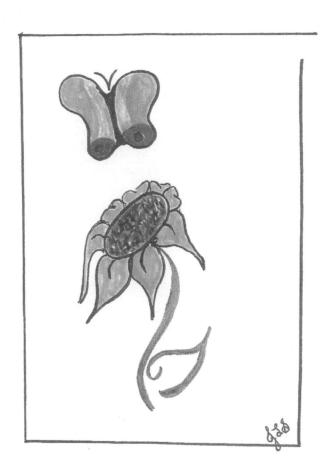

Karen Shipp RN, BSN, MS

Love and Loss:
A Guide to Family Healing
After the Loss of Your Baby

Copyright 2016 InnGage Solutions, LLC
All Rights Reserved

All rights reserved.   No part of this publication may be reproduced, stored in a retrieval system, or transmitted in any form, or by an means electronic, mechanical photocopy, recording or otherwise, without the prior permission of the artist/publisher.

.

CONTRIBUTING BLOGGERS

- Melissa Petersen, RNC, MSN, CNPPN – Chasing Rainbows, northsidepnl.blogspot.com
- Lanie – amourningmom.com
- Jeannie– lessonsfromportergray.blogspot.com
- Tim Nelson – fathersgrievinginfantloss.blogspot.com
- Lindsey– mommadale.wordpress.com
- Keshia– infantangel.wordpress.com
- Eileen Tully – littlewingedones.com
- Sandy Brosam – griefbeach.com
- Lori Ennis – stillstandingmag.com
- Katie – thelittlegreenfamily.blogspot.com
- Nan Zastrow – opentohope.com
- Katherine Reif-Canas – opentohope.com
- Alice Wisler – opentohope.com
- Harriet Hodgson – opentohope.com

EDITING SUPPORT

For their encouragement and assistance with the content and formatting of this book, my deepest gratitude goes to:

- Carol Shutley, CT
- Melissa Petersen, RNC, MSN, CNPPN

Special thanks go to Peter, Jennifer, and Kristin for their illustrations and photos.

DISCLAIMER

The blog postings and articles in Love & Loss are taken "as is" from each individual's website or publication and therefore express reality in their own uniquely individual ways.   We have not altered their original presentation in any way other than where we condensed for the sake of brevity.   Any condensations are indicated by the standard rules of composition.

A NOTE ABOUT THE BOOK

This book is in no way meant to replace guidance from your medical providers. In this book, we simply aim to give you and your family a place to begin processing what is happening to you, even in the midst of your grief. Any medical questions/concerns should be reported promptly to your provider.

Since you have all lost someone who lives still in your heart, and since we don't know whether your child is a boy or girl, or one of each, we have chosen to vary the wording when honoring your child's brief life. Therefore, we use "Him," Her," or 'Them" alternatively so we can celebrate and honor each life.

Many people have contributed to this book. Our common goal is to help you navigate the next days, months, and years. We want to thank the bereaved parents who have generously allowed us to use their writings for sharing moments of their own painful and personal journey on the road to healing.

We are all pulling for you.

4

A Message for You and Your Family

We're so sorry.

That's the only thing we can say - whether we have experienced a loss like yours or not. That's the only thing we can say.

Our hearts are with you. We want to help. The loss of a child is overwhelming and life changing.

We want to lend a shoulder and set your feet on the road to healing.

The next hours, days, weeks, and months are going to be **crazy, desperate, helpless, angry, guilt-ridden - challenging. They will be life-changing**.

There will be times when you don't know where to find the help you need.

This book is designed to give you information and resources over and above the things your caregiver gave you at the time of your loss. The first goal of your healthcare provider was to get you through the first few days. Now, we want to help you find a way forward.

You will find you need to sort, decipher - and eventually accept - the emotions and realities of your new world. Here, we give you people who've walked in your footsteps. We've also included a selection of resources - books, blogs, internet sites, support groups - which we hope will help you in your journey towards healing and acceptance.

This loss affects your entire family. We know you will never forget.

Love and Loss – About This Guide

Your voyage through this storm begins with a brief introduction to the emotional and physical effects of your loss. After that, we'd like you to hear other voices - from people who've walked in your footsteps. Occasionally we'll branch out, but mostly we'd like you to hear from people who've been there. They'll tell you how it was for them and how they began to cope and move towards healing and acceptance. They will also tell you that the pain never really goes away - it just changes.

With these blogs, quotations, poems, artwork, and articles, we hope you'll begin a personal journey. Different cultures view the loss of a child in different ways; rituals differ; spiritual beliefs clash or intersect. But every parent, in every part of the world, grieves the loss of a child - and honors that life in a very personal and emotional way. We want to help you find your own way to grieve and honor. You may find you need to write. You may find other ways to navigate this trip.

Don't grieve. Anything you lose comes around in another form.
Rumi

We want you to find whatever works for you. We just want you to make it.

The Ride of My Life
Northsidepnl.blogspot.com
Wednesday, March 13, 2013

I think most people who have experienced loss of any kind will agree that time seems to stand still. It is like your world just stops, but at the same time, the rest of the world continues moving. The earth still rotates on its axis. People continue to live, completely unaware that your world has come to a fast and grinding halt.

All of this has made me think of the emotions that come along with feeling so isolated and so shattered. Right after my loss, my emotions would run the gamut of devastated, anxious, panicked, fearful, and happy (yes, sometimes happy) all in a 5 minute time period. It has been 3 years and 3 months, and sometimes my emotions still are very unpredictable. I have heard grief described as "a roller coaster of emotions." Well, I guess I need to buckle up and prepare myself for the ride.

When I was a teenager, I remember going to Six Flags with some friends and riding that really old, wooden roller coaster the Scream Machine. To this day, I don't know what my feelings are about that ride....scary, exhilarating, stomach lurching terror. I remember that at one point, even though I was wearing my lap belt (that is all there is to keep you inside!), I felt like I was going to fly right out. I think that is what most people love about that ride, but it terrified me and I have always refused to ride it since.

I guess you could say that I have been riding a very similar roller coaster for the past 3 years. The difference is that I didn't buy a ticket for this one and stand in line for an hour to ride it. No, I just happened to walk right on, along with hundreds of other moms and dads who had to go home from the hospital without their babies. This ride is gut wrenching at times and has broken me down to the point of exhaustion before. It has brought me tears, anxiety, and has left me with a hole in my heart that can't be filled with anything else.

But I can't talk about this ride without acknowledging the beauty that has come from it. True--as awful as the loss of my baby daughter was and is for me, there is so much joy and beauty that comes with saying her name and talking about her story. Without her and her story, I would be a completely different person. This one tiny little person taught me compassion and dignity in a way that I could never have learned it otherwise. Her story is a part of me, just as I am a part of her.

I will probably be riding my roller coaster for some time. I still have a lot of healing left to do. And this is one of those rides that doesn't make you get off until you are good and ready. You see, I am in charge of my experience, just as you are in charge of yours. What we make of this ride is completely and utterly up to us. So, for now, I am going to tighten that lap belt a good bit tighter and keep my eyes wide open and maybe even hold my arms in the air so that I can really feel all the emotions and the world around me. This ride is mine. It may not be what I signed up for, but it is mine and my daughter's legacy will be waiting for me when I get off. So, I need to make my ride and my journey count. It's a daunting task, but an important one.

In the meantime, the world is still moving and is encouraging me to be a part of it.

Your personal journey may involve many different ways of showing your love and honoring your child.

So long as we live, they too shall live for they are now a part of us as we remember them.
Gates of Prayer,
Judaism Prayer Book

Your faith may play a vital role.

Blessed are those who mourn, for they will be comforted.
Matthew 5:4

You may find other pathways to peace and acceptance.

7

Whatever road you choose, this is a long trip. This loss will never go away. It will always remain in your heart. Our wish is that you find your own path, guided by others who have been there.

Our goal is for you to find the light at the end of the tunnel of your grief.

Remember, you're not alone. We can't change what's happened. Lots of us can't understand the depth of the confusing, frightening, devastating thing that happened to you. But we can offer you our support and love for as long as you need it.

Just as a little bird cracks open the shell and flies out, we fly out of this shell, the shell of the body. We all call that death, but strictly speaking, death is nothing but a change of form.

Swami Satchidananda

Table of Contents

Grief is like a ball of string, you start at one end and wind. Then the ball slips through your fingers and rolls across the floor. Some of your work is undone but not all. You pick it up and start over again, but you never have to begin again at the end of the string. The ball never completely unwinds. You've made progress.

Author Unknown

When you are sorrowful look again in your heart, and you shall see that in truth you are weeping for that which has been your delight.

Kahlil Gibran

Goodbyes are not forever. Goodbyes are not the end. They simply mean I'll miss you. Until we meet again.

Author Unknown

Table of contents

You will never forget this loss, but you can find a way to heal, accept, and honor. Your Walkabout begins now.

Part 1: **Understanding Grief**

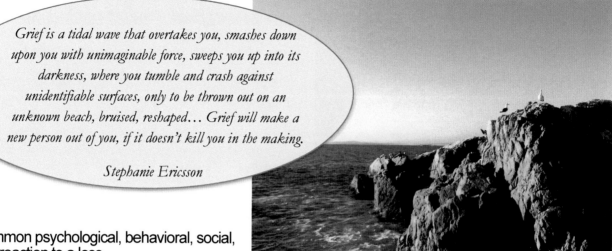

Grief is a tidal wave that overtakes you, smashes down upon you with unimaginable force, sweeps you up into its darkness, where you tumble and crash against unidentifiable surfaces, only to be thrown out on an unknown beach, bruised, reshaped... Grief will make a new person out of you, if it doesn't kill you in the making.

Stephanie Ericsson

Grief is a common psychological, behavioral, social, and physical reaction to a loss.

That doesn't mean there's anything uncomplicated or simple about it. It's a very complex process that can't be pinned down to any "right" or "wrong." It's overwhelming.

You may be in shock - numb, unable to concentrate. You can't eat or sleep. You avoid all social occasions or celebrations - certainly anything involving babies.

Where is your baby?

Sometimes you never got to look into his eyes.

Sometimes you got to spend a little time with them.

However it happened - she is still gone.

When the Walls Come Tumbling Down
www.amourningmom.com

As I wrote about here, the house where I was pregnant with Jake was sold a few months ago. We had a room for Jake in that house but he never came home to it. There was a time after Jake died that I had such anger towards that room. I wanted to renovate it, destroy it or at least move far, far away from it.

My anger was not rational but it seemed very real to me at the time. Along with denial, bargaining, depression and acceptance, anger is one of Elizabeth Kubler-Ross' 5 stages of grief. I guess I did not have anyone to be angry with so why not get mad at a room painted baby blue? So, when we sold that house we knew that it would most likely be torn down.

When I drove by a few days after the demolition began, there was only one room left standing...It is just Jake's room. Now the whole house is gone, but Jake will never be forgotten. We love you, Jake.

You try to make sense of what has happened. Sometimes you can find meaning through faith or circumstances that appear to you. It doesn't always make sense, and even "sense" doesn't change the fact that your child has died and that hurts so much.

Sometimes you had to make really hard decisions. The universe gave you a gift though, as "Lessons from Porter Gray" explains, you may not realize that at the time.

38 Minutes with Porter
lessonsfromportergray.blogspot.com

Even to your old age and gray hairs
I am he, I am he who will sustain you. I have made you and I will carry you;
I will sustain you and I will rescue you.
Isaiah 46:4

The verse from which this blog was named. It's been a week since Porter left my arms to be with my heavenly Father and I am holding to the truth that he is carrying me, sustaining me, and rescuing me in these difficult days.

We had 38 minutes to tell Porter how much we loved him, to kiss him and touch him while he was still with us. 38 minutes is 38 more than we were ever promised, but as any parent who's experienced the loss of a child will tell you it will never be enough.

I am convinced that every moment leading up to March 2nd was designed specifically by God to answer our prayers for time with Porter.

I was not scheduled to have another ultrasound with a doctor until the week before when we met with an OB that felt it would be of value. She immediately called to get us a consult while we were in the office with her. Prior to her, everyone essentially said it wasn't worth it since we were only going to provide comfort measures and it wouldn't change the outcome.

I went for this ultrasound and ended up being admitted for high blood pressure and to rule out preeclampsia (complications from pregnancy). While preeclampsia was ruled out, I happened to have another ultrasound that showed that my amniotic fluid was dangerously low (dangerous for Porter). The doctors, knowing that our wishes were to meet him and have time with him suggested we consider delivering him in the next day or two.

We chose to deliver him Friday, March 2nd. Porter's Birthday—a day I'll never forget. When Porter was born, our doctor said the umbilical cord was wrapped twice around his neck and was fairly tight. I believe fully that Porter would not have lasted another day if we had waited.

There were too many things that came together to bring Porter into the world on March 2nd for it to have been coincidence. I believe that even in this hardest of circumstances, God was answering our prayers and telling us we made the right decisions and gave us a gift. A gift of 38 minutes. I'll be honest with you though, I am so looking forward to eternity.

You have nightmares. You're angry and resentful - sometimes at inconvenient times. You're obsessed with "WHY?".

You think you're going crazy.

On the other hand, if you are sort of "crazy" right now - go with it.

It's OK to be "crazy" right now.

I try to take one day at a time, but sometimes several days attack me at once.

Ashleigh Brilliant

Recognize that on certain days the greatest grace is that the day is over and you get to close your eyes. Tomorrow comes more brightly

Mary Anne Radmacher

Grief is hard, but it's normal.

Why us?
Fathersgrievinginfantloss.blogspot.com

There was a new post yesterday under the Self-Esteem heading on this blog. As the dad mentioned, he was not sure he was necessarily facing a self-esteem issue, but was more struggling with the question of "why us?".

I certainly experienced the same feeling when Kathleen died. How can something like this happen to two people who wanted a baby so much? How can it happen to two people who are good parents and want to share their love with a child? How can it happen to people who have a belief system and try to live their lives accordingly? The questions can go on and on. I just wish that with the wisdom I have gained in the last 25 years I could say I have an answer, but I don't. I think the closest thing to an answer I can come up with is that there is no answer.

However, I can assure you that you are likely going to hear all sorts of theories from people who are trying to make you feel better. Things like, "it was meant to be," and "God has a plan for all of us," "there must have been something wrong," or, "you just have to try again." Again, the comments will go on and on. Keep in mind that most of those people are simply trying to find the same answers you are and are sincerely attempting to be helpful.

The dad who wrote the post also made comments about being angry with others who had children. He even mentioned feeling a sense of shame for being the father of a child who died. But it was his last sentence that really touched me. He said, "It is a helplessness that seems to be cruelly designed to crush a man." I have never had anyone so eloquently describe exactly how I felt at the time of our loss...helplessness cruelly designed to crush me.

With the benefit of time and healing on my side, I can see now that the helplessness, anger, and envy are all part of what we refer to as grief. They are just some of the emotions held in the grief capsule, and when we can express them, we are taking steps toward healing. I know that is of little consolation when you are in pain, but I hope you can find some hope in that.

Keep in mind that there is no right or wrong way to do this. But, there are some basic concepts:

Grief is not a disorder, a disease or a sign of weakness. It is an emotional, physical and spiritual necessity, the price to pay for love. The only cure for grief is to grieve.

Earl Grollman

- Acknowledge your grief for what it is - a normal reaction to loss.
- Find counseling - for yourself or your family. An objective listener often helps.
- Create memories. Honor your child. Name your child. You will never forget him.
- Take care of yourself. Pamper yourself. Yoga. Exercise. Nature.
- Find a support system - family, clergy, on-line blogs, support groups - your partner.
- Support each other. Remember you are both grieving - even if you each do it differently

Everyone handles grief differently. Let's look at those differences. Mothers, fathers, siblings, grandparents, friends - all are going to be affected by this loss. Look at the different ways your family is going to experience this horrible storm. Listen to the voices of people who understand.

A. Mothers

When you lose your baby, a part of you dies. You have known this child for days, weeks, months. You know your child's heartbeat as well as you know your own.
Ultrasound pictures, hearing the heartbeat - all a miracle.

You rejoiced.

She is gone.

You're empty and alone.

> **It went by too fast**
> Mommadale.wordpress.com
> Posted on June 11, 2013

It has been exactly 14 days since we held our son, kissed him, smelled him. I cry every day…every single day. It comes out of nowhere and hits me like a freight train. Last week I couldn't get out of bed without crying for a good 10 minutes. This week I haven't cried when I wake up but have managed to cry myself to sleep several times, or worked my way into one of those cries where you can't catch your breath and your nose is so stuffed up that you can't breathe through it. I cried last week when we watched tv and had cooked our first meal because that was something we always did and it didn't feel the same without him there. I cried when I thought about doing pizza movie Friday night as that is a tradition in our house and he loved pizza movie Friday night. I cried when I went to the grocery store yesterday because when I passed the juice boxes, I thought to myself, " I will never be able to make Asher's lunch for school." Grief is a biotch, no other way to put it. It comes on suddenly, when you are least expecting it.

If you lost her early, it's like no one noticed.

You did.

If you lost him later, no one knows how to respond.

Neither do you.

If you lost them days or weeks after birth, you found lots of love and sympathy. But few people really knew how to talk to you.

You're not even sure how to talk to yourself. Listen to Mommadale. She's angry, but she has to keep reminding herself that it's OK to be angry. At this point in your grieving, tell yourself anything you need to hear to just keep going.

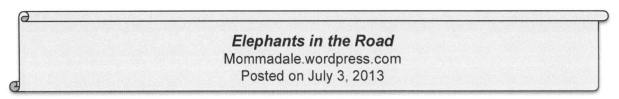

Elephants in the Road
Mommadale.wordpress.com
Posted on July 3, 2013

I have found myself really trying my best to feel "good" this past week. Last Wednesday was hard as it was Asher's one month mark, so as you can imagine I cried most of the day away thinking of what should have been. So, I did my best to do something to make me feel good, so I made several memorial boxes for the hospital. I had decided a few weeks ago that I wanted to try and help someone going through what I went through but I don't really have any talents. I came to the decision to put my efforts into creating personalized memorial boxes in honor of Asher. Families that lose a child get one of these that hold their baby's foot/ hand molds, lock of hair, blanket, arm bands, etc. It makes me feel like I am giving back in a way. So I made a few last Wednesday. Yeah, didn't work. I was still aching. Then I proceeded to go to the store to buy Asher's 1 month balloon, and got in front of a man who was homeless. He was trying to buy several things for a kitty cat along with some basic hygiene items but he did not have enough money. He started putting things back so I felt a tug on my heart to pay for the gentleman's items. If you know me, you know I am an animal lover so it broke my heart to see him pull out his wallet, which by the way was made of duct tape, to do his best to spend what little money he had on a cat. So I paid for his belongings and you could tell he was so thankful. It made me feel good for about 16.7 seconds until I got into my car and then the tears came yet again. Nothing seems to fill the void where Asher was. No parties, no dinner dates, no paying it forward, no running again, no work success. It seems to all be temporary. I feel like I am distracting myself from the reality of the situation and that is….. he was taken too soon.

…………………

I write all of this because so many friends, family and even strangers say how STRONG I am, how INSPIRATIONAL I am and how I am a TESTAMENT of what Faith looks like. Truth is, I am grieving. I am surviving but it is not without constant pain, doubt and anger. I want someone reading this that is going through a struggle to know I am right there with you. It's possible to survive the unimaginable but don't pressure yourself to be "okay" if you don't want to. Don't feel like being pissed off or having doubt makes you regret the decision you made. Just because I feel like my insides are empty does not mean I regret having Asher. Absolutely not. Just because I disagree with God taking my son away from me doesn't mean I don't have Faith. God expects us to ask questions…to be angry …to grieve. But do what I am doing and allow yourself to FEEL ALL OF IT- every emotion. I have to remind myself every day that it is okay to hate this situation. It is okay to hate the cards you were dealt. Trust me, if it was up to me, I would FIRE this dealer. I wish we weren't living this now. But we are and reality is, we have to live and work and function. I am slowly doing that, but it's not without bumps in the road bumps the size of elephants.

"Blessed are those who mourn, for they shall be comforted"……
Mathew 5:4

No one ever told me that grief felt so much like fear.

C.S. Lewis

Even your body is betraying you. It keeps doing its thing - preparing for the baby, triggering huge hormonal changes, getting ready to feed your child.

You think you need to be strong, but you have no control. Crying is all you can do. What happened? Why doesn't anyone understand? Why do they all have that pitying look and "Are you OK?" question in their eyes?

Can't they see you're not OK?

You're exhausted. Your world crashed.

Your family will never be the same and you don't know how to manage. You're too tired to cope right now.

We adapt, we accept, but we never get over it! I am often asked when will the pain pass away. My honest answer is never. It changes intensity like waves in the ocean…

Author Unknown

Things will change.

With time, your body and mind will adapt to your new normal. You'll reorder all the plans you made. You'll move on. You and your family will find ways to reconnect and support each other. But you will never forget.

The Butterfly Effect
northsidepnl.blogspot.com
Posted on January 17, 2014

Butterflies. They are a symbol of hope and peace. A symbol of rebirth and of the soul living on. Dr. Elizabeth Kubler- Ross was a doctor known for her work with death and dying. I am a nurse and am very familiar with Kubler-Ross's stages of grief. Dr. Kubler-Ross wrote a book, The Wheel of Life, A Memoir of Living and Dying, about her post war visit to the site of the Maidanek concentration camp, which is in Poland. She spent time in the area where the children had lived and she saw clothing and shoes and the signs that they had been there. And then she saw the butterflies. They had been carved into the walls with pebbles and fingernails. There were hundreds of them. Twenty-five years later, after listening to hundreds of terminally ill patients, she came to the realization that the prisoners in the camps must have known that they were going to die. "They knew that soon they would become butterflies. Once dead, they would be out of that hellish place. Not tortured anymore. Not separated from their families. Not sent to gas chambers. None of this gruesome life mattered anymore. Soon they would leave their bodies the way a butterfly leaves its cocoon. And I realized that was the message they wanted to leave for future generations. . . .It also provided the imagery that I would use for the rest of my career to explain the process of death and dying."

Butterflies. I don't know if I have written yet about the butterfly that followed me one day, shortly after my Elizabeth was stillborn. She was born in December, which is not the season for butterflies. But, one came to me just after Christmas, on a day that I was feeling especially sad. Just out of the blue, it flew around me, getting really close to me. I didn't think too much of it at first. To be honest, I really didn't think of much at all then. I was just blank, pretty void of all feeling for a while. I went through the day just waiting to go to bed, so that I could forget about how much I hurt.

My butterfly didn't waiver. It stayed with me for a while. I am not sure how long, but it was long enough for me to finally take notice that it was odd to see a butterfly in the middle of winter. I don't know if you believe in messages, but I do. I think that beautiful little creature was a message to me from my sweet girl. She woke me up out of the fog. That butterfly got me outdoors for a little while each day, in hopes that I would see it again. It lifted the fog which had become my everyday so that I could hope for a little more.

In hindsight, I guess you can say it was the start of the long healing journey that I am still on. This week, I have thought a lot of my butterfly and of the butterflies that were drawn on the walls in Poland by those dear children. I have seen other butterflies, some of whom lingered and made me smile, but none like that one. What amazing creatures they are to inspire those precious children in the Maidanek camp to dream of hope and the desire to share that message for the future. Such an incredible creature....so incredible that it has become a symbol of hope for dying people and for those like us in the babyloss community who wake up every single day missing our little children. Those of us who are searching for something to show us how to spread our wings and fly again, amidst all the sadness, in the hopes of finding our own "new normal."

B. Fathers

As a father, you're going to find your own unique struggles.

Your first concern is for the mother of your child. Is she OK? How can you make this better and protect her?
It's your responsibility to be strong and fix everything. Isn't it?
What did you do wrong?

> *Be patient with yourself. Be patient with your partner. But do not run the other direction or try to hide. It doesn't work – I have already tried. I wish you well.*
>
> *Tim Nelson*

Tim Nelson shares his struggle with guilt, helplessness, and need for control following the death of his daughter.

Trying to control the uncontrollable...
Fathersgrievinginfantloss.blogspot.com

Thinking back, I realize now that much of my behavior in the early hours after finding out that our daughter was dead, was the result of my need to stay in control. Throughout my life, I had come to believe that staying in control of situations and my life represented strength and the path to success.

I believed that staying focused on school work and doing my best would mean that I got into a good college, and eventually landed a job that made me good money and earned me the respect of my family and peers. To a large extent, I still believe that to be true. What I did not realize at the time, was that there were situations in life I could not control.

Even though I seemed to be living the American dream by doing well in school, graduating from a good college, starting my own business, marrying my high school sweetheart, buying a home, and starting a family after 5 years of marriage -- I could not stop my daughter from dying.

There was no preparing me for facing that reality. When I found out that our baby was dead, life as I knew it began to unravel. My first thought was that my "secrets" had finally caught up with me. Maybe the college partying had taken more of a toll than I realized. Maybe God was punishing me for thoughts that I had had or lies I had told.

When the guilt set in, I tried all that much harder to control what I could. I would not allow myself to cry -- therefore I avoided situations that might make me cry. I hurried along our time alone with Kathleen because I feared the longer I was with her, the harder it would be to say goodbye. I chose to let the hospital handle her remains, because I could not fathom going to her funeral. I didn't want to have a lot of family around at the hospital because I didn't want them to see me so vulnerable.

In other words, I was out of control. When the feelings of fear and sadness blended together, my behavior made it seem like I cared much less than I did. I think it's for this reason that I always point out to moms that they need to be careful not to judge their partner's feelings by their behavior. The old, "you can't judge a book by it's cover," adage rings real true in circumstances like these -- especially for men.

19

You failed at a primary task. You couldn't protect your child.

That's what Dads do. Right? They Protect.

Sure, you didn't carry this baby, but you connected - maybe not as early as your partner, maybe not until you heard a heartbeat - but you connected. You loved. You dreamed. You wanted to protect.

You are a Father. Yet you couldn't protect him.

In "A Father's Story," Rabbi David J. B. Krishef addresses the overwhelming sense of guilt that he felt when his baby girl died and how his beliefs helped him cope.

Anything that's human is mentionable, and anything that is mentionable can be more manageable. When we can talk about our feelings, they become less overwhelming, less upsetting, and less scary. The people we trust with that important talk can help us know that we are not alone.

Fred Rogers

A Father's Story
By Rabbi David J.B. Krishef
In memory of our daughter, Bracha Pela, zikhrona livraka
Ncjh.org/downloads/OAfall2010.pdf

Tuesday, July 23, 1996, was the night our sons Solomon and Zachary, and their sister Bracha were born. It was the same night the doctors told us that our daughter had only a slim chance of living out the week. It was also the night on which the Jewish traditions concerning the beginning and the end of life came into sharp focus for me. That night, the halachic/legal writings of Rabbis Dorff and Reisner regarding the cessation of ventilation for the terminally ill echoed in my mind and in my heart. Our beautiful little daughter was dying, and by 6:00 a.m. on the morning after she was born, the doctors explained that she had no chance of surviving, and that the ventilator was merely prolonging her death, rather than extending her life. In such a case it is permitted to remove the ventilator, and let death take its' natural course.

I wept over our daughter's bed for hours the night she and her brothers were born, and I apologized to her for the pain that I, through her conception, had caused. I asked her to watch over her brothers, and give them strength, and I asked her brothers to be strong, and through their presence in our life, help us to make it through the coming hours and days. We held Bracha in our arms as she died the next morning-we kissed her and we comforted her. I can only pray that her death was made easier, less painful as a result of having two loving parents hold her at the end, rather than letting her lie alone in a neonatal intensive care unit under bright lights, connected to loudly beeping machines by innumerable tubes and wires, as she felt nurses forcefully pumping oxygen into her malformed lungs through a hard plastic ventilator tube.

After Bracha Pela died, I asked the nurse for a pair of scissors, ripped my shirt and said the berakha, "Barukh dayan ha'emet, "Blessed is the righteous Judge." I made one call, to the Hevra Kadisha/Burial society, which made all arrangements for Bracha's burial. I did not want to see or speak to anyone at that point except my immediate family. Never have I appreciated the halakha of death and dying more than on the days which followed it gave me comfort and structure at a time when my life was cold and chaotic. Our Jewish traditions provided a way to receive support and understanding amidst the most inexplicable of all sorrows - the loss of a baby.

You're mad. You're just plain angry. You're in pain. But you can't show it.

You have to be strong.

You have other children. How do you tell them their new brother or sister isn't coming home?

You're dealing with "The Family" because your partner can't and you have to be sure she's OK.

Finally, after all of that, you're angry with people you feel let you down. In "The gift of forgiveness," Tim Nelson addresses this anger and describes how forgiveness can be turned into a means of regaining some sense of control.

The gift of forgiveness
Fathersgrievinginfantloss.blogspot.com

It is rare that I am home watching TV on a Friday night (we are firm believers in trying to kick off the week-end with a diversion), but last night I found myself watching Dateline for the first time in a year. The program was depressing, . . . It was about a man and woman (brother and sister) who, as teenagers in 1979, were the victims of a home invasion. Their father . . . and their mother were both senselessly murdered in the random attack. The children both survived, although they were critically wounded. The Dateline report was about . . . how they eventually began to heal and were able to move forward. While the experience will obviously impact them the rest of their lives, the real focus of the story became the young man's ability to forgive the person who pulled the trigger that horrendous night. A lot of the questions to him centered around, "how could you possibly forgive someone who did that?"

What struck me in all the questions and answers about forgiveness was that no one ever mentioned that forgiveness does not mean condoning the hurtful action that occurred. The (Grief Recovery) Institute's philosophy is that forgiveness really means, "I am not going to let this hurt me anymore." By looking at it that way, it gives at least a minuscule piece of responsibility (and control) to the person who feels they have been wronged. It becomes their decision as to how they want to move forward.

I was very angry at a certain individual caregiver who failed us when Kathleen died. I could not have been convinced at the time that there was any way I could forgive him. When I started to look at forgiveness as setting myself free rather than letting him totally off the hook, I was better able to let go and move on.

At this point, you're convinced you have to be strong. You can't cry; crying is weak and weakness is not what your partner or your family needs.

You feel you *have to be strong. Wrong.*

Relationships - Maria
facesofloss.com/real-advice/relationships#more-2332

Through trials in our marriage DH and I have built strong communication skills, which was so crucial after our loss. I knew I could share with him any feeling, no matter how irrational, and he was going to be sympathetic to that. On the flip side I was fortunate enough to have him share with me, he very honestly told me how hard it was for him to see me hurting and know that he could not run in and save the day. At their very core, men are heroes and problem solvers and in the case of the loss they, really can't be either, it just doesn't work that way with child loss. It was so important for me to assure my husband that no, he could not fix our miscarriage or take the hurt away, but that him being there to hold me, and cry with me was enough…and he has been!

Remember...

It's OK to grieve. It's OK to cry. It's OK to talk about your feelings with your partner. It's OK to be afraid and sad.

You don't have to be "Mr. Fix It."

Find ways to work out your feelings. Exercise. Do yard work. Do whatever works. Do what you need to do.

Spend "alone time" as you need.

Spend time with your partner.

You'll work together to navigate your grief. Let her know you are hurting too. She needs to know that — almost as much as she needs to know you are there to lean on. Together you'll come through this.

A Man in Grief

It must be very difficult to be a man in grief.
Since "men don't cry" and "men are strong"
No tears can bring relief.

It must be very difficult to stand up to the test
And field the calls and visitors so she can get
some rest.

They always ask if she's all right and ask what
she's going through,
But seldom take his hand and ask, "My friend, but
how are you?"

He hears her crying in the night and thinks his
heart will break.
He dries her tears and comforts her, but stays
"strong" for her sake.

It must be very difficult to start each day anew
and try to be so very brave. He lost his
baby, too.

Eileen Knight Hagemeister

In the end, "it just takes time."

"It just takes time..."
Fathersgrievinginfantloss.blogspot.com

I was on the Compassionate Friends Facebook page and noticed that someone had posted a question/comment about "time healing all wounds." The reaction from other parents was pretty strong, and quite

universal in expressing that time indeed does NOT heal all wounds. . . .

For me, the question really comes down to what is healing vs. accepting the new reality? Acceptance, in my book, does not necessarily mean healing, but rather coming to a point where a bereaved person realizes that no amount of sadness, anger, or hopelessness is going to make things different and the process of grieving allows them to start moving forward again.

In other words, it is not TIME itself that helps, but rather what you DO WITH THE TIME. If you curl up in a ball, pull the shades, and let your sadness take over, no days, weeks, or months off the calendar are going to help make you feel better. But if you use that grieving time to reflect and express your sadness and anger in a healthy way so the pressure does not become unbearable, life can become worth living again.

Believe me, it is not that I don't understand that sometimes the sadness is so overwhelming it seems completely impossible to ever think of being happy again. But, I also don't believe that we are dishonoring our children and the love we feel for them by allowing ourselves to smile, be happy, and feel hope.

We had started to call him "quarterback" because he was unbelievably active. I was really looking forward to playing ball with him when he was older. Now, I hate to see a guy playing with his kids.

"Healing Together"
A Centering Corporation Resource, by Marcie Lister and Sandra Lovell

---

"Dad and Father"
www.amourningmom.com
Evan, October 2013 Walk to Remember speech

I am the father of four children,
but I am "Dad" to only two kids.

Our six-year-old twins call me "Dad" or "Daddy"
– or sometimes other silly things, or things I won't mention here.

Our first child, Jake, never left the hospital
and lived only 2 weeks.
He was born 14 weeks early
and with other ultimately unsolvable medical complications.

Our fourth child, Sawyer, was born happy and healthy
and came home with us.
But six weeks later, with no warning,
and for no reason that has yet been fully figured out,
his heart stopped working.

Neither Jake nor Sawyer ever got to call me anything.

My family and I grieve the deaths and loss of our boys,
as you all grieve the loss of your children and little loved-ones.

As their father, I grieve the loss of Jake and Sawyer's childhoods,
the big moments that they were supposed to have but never will.
I grieve the loss of their chance to grow up, to flourish,
to become teenagers, young men, husbands and "Dads" themselves.
I grieve the lost ball games and trips and adventures we'll never have.
I grieve all the missed hugs and high-fives.
I grieve even the cranky wake-ups and bedtime fits we know so well from our twins,
but never got to experience with Jake or Sawyer.

I grieve all the truly heart-warming bedtime snuggles
that will never happen with Jake or Sawyer.
Beyond all those missed tender moments,
I also grieve the loss of my belief that horrible things won't happen to me or my loved ones.
I am all too aware now that they can happen to anyone – as they have happened to all of us.

It's all I can do most of the time
to just hope nothing like losing Jake and Sawyer ever happens again.
As a father, I also grieve the loss of my once unshakable belief
that I could always protect my wife Lanie and all our children
from such terrible pain and anguish; that I can "fix" their problems;
that I can always make everything all better.

I know that I cannot make Jake or Sawyer all better or bring them back.
I'm not sure that grief is something a father can ever overcome.
Of course, I have learned that you do not overcome or get past grief.
You just go through it.
I hate that my family has to go through it too,
but thank heavens I have an incredible wife and wonderful kids
to travel along with me as I go down that path.

So I guess I will always grieve the loss of never being called "Dad" –
not even once – by Jake or Sawyer.

But that doesn't mean I am not their father.
I am and always will be a proud father of all my kids,
no matter what they call me
or what they were never able to call me.

C. Couples

Let's look at how this loss is going to affect you as a couple.

Lots of people think losing a child brings a couple closer together. Sometimes that's not the case.

BUT

There are things you can do to help each other which will bring you out the other end stronger, more together, more understanding, and more loving.

What is Love?
Northsidepnl.blogspot.com
Posted on February 19, 2014

I read such a great article today. It was an article that was about love and Valentine's Day. The Huffington Post had asked for people to send in pictures that depicted true love. Someone had sent in a picture of herself and her partner in the hospital on the day that her daughter was born still. The picture is not a picture of what most would consider lovely. It is certainly not a happy picture. It is a picture of two parents grieving together. Loving their daughter together. Being together.

When I saw the picture and read the article, there were several things that came into my mind. One was an image of my husband. My quiet, wonderful, six foot three inch tall, past-football playing husband silently binding my breasts after our Elizabeth was born still. That remains, in my mind, one of the most powerful experiences of my life. I remember that he cried as he wrapped the tight bandage around my breasts and helped me put the cabbage leaves in. I had so much milk coming in. I remember him saying how wrong it was that she would not be able to drink it. It was my birthday. And when he was finished, he said, "I am sorry your birthday can not be happy." It was the most masculine thing he has ever done. It was also the most loving.

So, how do you love, protect, and cherish your relationship?

First: Honor your relationship

You are important as a couple. Keep a weekly date night. Remember how you met, how your love developed. Check in with each other on a regular basis. Daily? Hourly? Whatever you need.

Hold each other. Cry together if it feels right. It's certainly OK.

The first time we walked into the baby's room both of us were crying. It was very difficult…the pad on the dresser, the stuffed duck, things around the room. We just started gathering up things and taking them down to the basement. We stood there and looked at each thing, then put it in a trunk. I guess this was our version of a funeral. We put the lid back on the trunk, pushed it back where it belonged, and held each other.

A Father's Grief: RTS Bereavement Services

Relationships - Jamie

facesofloss.com/real-advice/relationships#more-2332

I've been blessed to share my life with a wonderful man. Sometimes we just need to sit together in silence, almost as a moment of understanding. On the random occasion when I walk up to him crying, he doesn't even ask what's wrong, he just puts his arms around me and holds me tight. We're so in tune that the times we have that silent moment, we just know. I guess it's been a confirmation of what doesn't kill us makes us stronger. Thank God for that & for him. I don't know what I'd do without that.

Second: Accept each other's limitations and different grieving styles

Give each other room to grieve as an individual. Remember, there is no right or wrong way to do this.

Relationships - Jennifer

facesofloss.com/real-advice/relationships#more-2332

My husband and I are closer since we lost our 5 month old son in September. One very important thing we've realized is that we grieve differently, and we have to support that in each other.

Third: Refuse to play "the blame game"

This is the time to stand together in love and support. Try not to bring up old issues. Remember you both loved her, though you may show it in different ways.

Fourth: Be patient and don't be afraid to ask for help

You may grieve at different speeds. There is no right or wrong. If your partner needs longer, try to give him or her whatever time is needed. If that's hard for you, find someone else to talk with about your feelings. Look for support groups where you will be around people who understand what you are going through, both individually and as a couple.

He changed all the doorknobs in the house. We have new doorknobs on every door. He changed the outlets. We have new outlets and switches. He painted all the ceilings. How many people have all new doorknobs and outlets?

A Father's Grief: RTS Bereavement Services

Fifth: Talk about what happened

Sometimes all it takes is an honest conversation. Respect and honor each other's feelings and don't be afraid to voice them. Darkness is much more harmful than anything brought into the light.

Relationships - Patty
facesofloss.com/real-advice/relationships#more-2332

The first few weeks after we lost Stella we were closer than ever. As the weeks have passed (almost 4 months now) our relationship is strained. While I still have more sad/depressed times, he buries it deep inside. Counseling is helping us to bridge that gap though and we are both determined to work through this. Guys are just raised to be strong (from women) and when we are hurting and see them carrying on almost like nothing happened it creates a lot of anger, anger that they are not grieving like we are.

With time and space you may find, as Infantangel did: "...now I know at least part of the purpose of Lauren's short life. She strengthened the love between her parents, taught us a lot about things we didn't even know we needed to learn, and led us back to God."

One year
Infantangel.wordpress.com
Posted August 4, 2013

One year has passed since I became a mother. I always imagined that day would be a memorable one. It was certainly memorable, but not for all the reasons I thought it'd be. Because on that day I also earned the title bereaved parent. I became part of a community of people who live day to day with a pain that cannot be described. I've learned a lot about myself in the year that has passed since I met and said goodbye to my daughter. I've learned that I can apparently take anything that's thrown at me. I've learned that the love a mother feels for her children is a love that cannot be put into words.

When Lauren was born I wasn't surprised when I didn't hear her cry. I knew my girl was not ready to be born. My thoughts were of nothing but what that NICU team was doing to her and if it was going to help her at all. Of course it didn't. And in the hours following her death, when people were coming in the room to see us, I wasn't thinking of the joyful things a new mommy usually thinks of. My mind was filled with the thought that I'd never again get pregnant because there was no way I could go through that pain again. And thoughts of 'now what'. How do you process what has happened right after your newborn dies? I was wondering what we'd do as far as cremation funeral. I was wondering if my body was going to recover from the havoc caused by the preeclampsia. Nothing but negative thoughts…almost. One thing I did think of was a conversation my husband and I had right after we found out we were pregnant 6 months earlier. I'd told him that I really wished my Granny Hitt was still alive to meet her. So in the hours following her death, I thought, well, Lauren gets to be with Granny before any of us do. And my dad even mentioned it to me in the hospital room, a small sliver of light on such a dark week.

So as we acknowledge today, Lauren's birthday and the day she died, I am of course still sad. I will always be sad that my first born didn't get to live for more than 22 minutes. I am of course still angry some days. But a year has allowed me to learn so much about me, my husband, and other people in our lives. We've become stronger as a married couple and stronger in our faith. They say every life has a purpose and I've always believed that.

And now I know at least part of the purpose of Lauren's short life. She strengthened the love between her parents, taught us a lot about things we didn't even know we needed to learn, and led us back to God. And for that I'll be forever thankful. Happy Birthday in Heaven baby girl.

Sixth: Honor your child as a couple

Talk together about your individual experiences of their lives. Honor your family's lost dreams.

I think my grief was a little bit different than my wife's. My wife had nine months of attachment that I didn't have. I was looking forward to the day the twins would be born. My wife was able to enjoy the nine months prior to that.

A Father's Grief: RTS Bereavement Services

Work together to create memories and a legacy of his place in your family. Amourningmom tells us what worked for her.

How to Remember Your Child
www.amourningmom.com
Posted February 28, 2014

I will always remember Jake and Sawyer. How they looked. How they smelled. Their sounds, and the touch of their skin.

Over the years since Jake and then Sawyer have died, we've always looked for ways to remember them by trying to build more memories of them. Maybe it is because we only had weeks with each of them. Maybe it is because it is a way to keep them a more active part of our lives. Maybe it is because that is what we do when our loved ones are no longer present in our lives.

We've done things that have made sense to us to remember Jake and Sawyer. I've also come across suggestions (some of which we have taken, some of which we haven't done) from other resources about ways parents can remember their children who have died. Some of those ideas include:

- Create a baby album with all your keepsakes in it. (This might take different shapes or forms depending on what keepsakes you have.)
- Make a collage frame, remembrance or shadow box with pictures, mementos and other things that remind you of your child.
- Plant flowers or a tree in your child's memory, perhaps in a place you like to visit or that you associate with your child.
- Participate in walks or runs in your community.
- Buy memorial bricks (local parks often offer this as a fundraiser).

- Name a star after your baby.
- Write.
- Light candles.
- Volunteer or work on a special project in your child's memory.
- Donate to a child who would be the same age as your child would be.

Seventh: Allow laughter into your life; have fun

Your child wouldn't want you to be sad forever. It'll probably feel strange and you may feel a little guilty if you relax and enjoy a dinner, a sunset, the sight of the ocean. But it's OK. This is part of remembering, accepting, and healing.

Eighth: Stay healthy

Remember, your physical health is just as important as your emotional health. If possible, find some activity you can do together. It may be hard at first, but it's difficult to stay depressed when you're physically active. Whether you walk, run, bike, or work out, exercise will ease some of your anger and depression. You may discover sleep comes more easily and your connection with your partner in a loving relationship suddenly becomes easier and more spontaneous.

D. Siblings

Other family members are going to be affected by her death.

What do you say to your
other children?

Children's questions are a window to their soul – a mirror to their inner thoughts and feelings.

Great Answers to Difficult Questions about Death - What Children Need to Know

By Linda Goldman

Often, what you do or don't say depends on the age of your other children. Your toddler won't understand the finality of death. Your young child may picture a "Boogey Man" who can be outsmarted if he only knew how. Young children, still in the "magical thinking" stage of development may feel responsible for the loss of their brother or sister. Older children usually understand death and may even begin developing their own spiritual beliefs.

Don't be afraid of the word "death." Tell them their brother or sister died. Death is a reality and labeling it any other way leads to confusion and doesn't do justice to your child's ability to understand and adjust.

You'll probably find that your children return again and again with questions about death as they get older.

It's OK. It's normal. It's part of their growth.

For more information on children's grief, see "Responding to Children's Questions About Death" in the Appendix of this book.

Brigid's Eulogy
Littlewingedones.wordpress.com

As I knelt in prayer at church this past Sunday, I pondered Brigid's death, as I have done every second of each day since it happened.

Specifically, I thought about God as our Father and the giver of every good and perfect gift, who tells us that if we as parents know how to give good gifts to our children, how much more will he give good gifts to us if we ask him.

And I wondered: What about this? How is this a good gift?

I've told our boys that just because Brigid died, it does not mean that God didn't hear our daily prayers for her to grow big and strong and come home to live with us. "Sometimes," I told them, "God tells us no just like sometimes Mommy tells you no when you ask for things." They accepted that explanation…but I wasn't so sure I did.

We all tell our children no when there are things that they want that are not good for them, but as a mother, I tried to imagine the circumstances under which I could possibly tell my children no for something that would break their hearts as much as Brigid's death has broken ours. Why would I tell them no for something that would make them happy? What would have been the harm in allowing us to bring our healthy daughter home to live with our family? Especially after we'd already lost her sister.

I racked my brain for an example.

It came. It involved chocolate. And I realized that it all has to do with perspective.

I imagined myself baking in my kitchen. I love to make special things for my family, and I imagined I was making an extra special dessert treat for the birthday party of one of my boys. Only he didn't know I was doing it for him.

He comes into the kitchen where I am standing and asks if he can have a few of the chocolate chips that are on the counter. Because I need to use them for the dessert, I tell him no.

Being the young child he is, he is devastated. "Please, please, please?" he pleads. "Trust me," I say. "No."

He falls to the floor crying and kicking and screaming. But I do not change my answer. Instead, I lovingly pick him up, give him a hug, and tell him to go and let me work. He doesn't know it, but within a short time, I'll have used the chocolate chips to create something extra special for his party, and I know that he will love it. This is why I can be a loving parent and yet be unmoved by his pleas.

And then I thought about this example in terms of my perspective on our situation.

To a young child, my denying him the treat that he wanted was devastating. But as his mother, I knew I had a plan for it that was far better. I knew his tears would be short-lived, but that he'd appreciate the final product much more than the chips by themselves.

To him, the few hours until the party seemed like an eternity. But to me, it was just a brief wait that was worthwhile for the celebration that was to come.

The small chocolate chips would have been a treat for him and they would have made him happy, but the special dessert would serve many more people and benefit him as well as others.

I have to think that our Father, with his infinite knowledge, sees our situation in much the same way that I, as a mother, see things in relation to our boys.

Our wait to see Brigid and Fiona again is nothing more to him than a little boy's wait for his birthday celebration. But oh, the celebrating will be so much greater. The pain of being denied our request feels profound and deep; our tears will flow for months instead of minutes. But to our Father, this is but a short-lived trial. Our girls would have enriched and blessed our family had we been able to bring them home to live with us, but incorporated into his plan, they have been used to affect so many others.

Many of you might never have known about our twin girls were this not the plan. And I'm pretty certain that none of us will ever be the same again. We prayed and we rejoiced and we prayed and we cried. Our prayers brought us to our knees in the middle of the night. They drew us in close to the God who was in control of this situation from the very start. They came from Australia and China and Hungary and Canada and Scotland. They came from people who were prayer warriors and from people who had never prayed before. They brought glory to God because they made us acknowledge the frailty and wonder of life and realize that there is a power greater than us at work.

To know that our girls may have been used as part of God's plan for someone else is humbling. Our faith has not been shaken by their death. Rather, it has been toned and stretched and strengthened. We have been brought to the end of ourselves and found that He still gave us the strength to go on. Our prayers for Fiona and for Brigid were really for our benefit too. The act of praying for them tested us and helped us to grow stronger. And though God chose to answer our prayers with "no," our prayers were not in vain.

Copyright 2013 Eileen Tully. Used with permission from the author.

Keep in mind.

While children may not say anything, they're always watching and they'll pick up on family tension. They know you're sad. They may want to "fix" things. Explain that while they can't "fix" this any more than you can, there may be some ways they can help and then help them with whatever plan they come up with.

Remember, they are also grieving. Honor their feelings and allow them to grieve in their own way, just as you are grieving in yours.

A child can live with anything as long as he or she is told the truth and is allowed to share with the loved ones the natural feelings people have when they are suffering.

Eda LeShane

What matters is that you involve them. Answer their questions honestly. Use simple, direct answers that acknowledge their age and ability to understand death.

Don't be afraid to say you don't know the answer to their questions.

Use language, art - and hugs. Let them express their thoughts and feelings. Be sure they know you are there. Tell them you'll be there. Their world will go on.

A Mourning Mom

...*"People who love each other are always connected by a very special String made of love."*

"But if you can't see it, how do you know it's there?" asked Liza.

"Even though you can't see it with your eyes, you can feel it with your heart and know that you are always connected to everyone you love."
....

"Does the String go away when you're mad at us?"

"Never," said Mom. "Love is stronger than anger, and as long as love is in your heart, the String will always be there."

The Invisible String
Patrice Karst
Copyright 2000
DeVorss & Company, Publishers

Never assume that saying nothing is the best way to protect your children from sadness or loss.

Sandy Brosam shares her special ritual on GriefBeach.com.

Angel Hugs
Griefbeach.com/angel-hugs/
Sandy Brosam

When I was starting my grief journey, I had to teach myself and my children how to cope with the pain on a daily basis. I had to make the statement, "he's right here in your heart" real to myself and my children. I did this with my Angel Hug.

Angel Hugs:

For myself: I would find a quiet place where I felt safe to just be in the moment. Then I would take my arms and open them up at my sides, and open my clutched fists, and pull my arms into my chest, crossing them over my heart. I would close my eyes, and calm my thoughts. I would visualize a white light of healing energy and love coming down from above, swirling around me. I would just let go and feel this energy, and think of my son's love, and feel it enter my heart where the emptiness was. I would visualize it as a pulsating force of love, and as the love came in, it pushed the pain out the bottom of my feet into the earth to be dispelled. When I felt the pulsating stop, I would open my eyes, and I would feel amazing! I would be relaxed, peaceful, and the tears would be gone. We are never alone, we just have to let the love in!

I still do this, even 30 years into my grief journey. I have developed a "quickie" for myself, when out in public. We all have emotional "triggers" that sneak up on us at the worst times…so I can reach up and place my hand over my heart, just for a moment, and give myself a mini hug. People think I have heartburn (yeah you could call it that) or I am going to burp…but what I am doing is reminding myself of the love to push the pain away. It allows me to stay composed in public.

For my children: I would sit or stand behind them, (ages 3 and 8 when I taught them) and have them cross their hearts with open hands, and wrap my arms around them crossing their heart also. I would talk them thru the visualization, and help them to learn how to do this themselves. We would feel the love together, and push the pain out together. We grieved together.

You can call it God's Love, Angel's Love, Spirit's Love…I just call it LOVE, and it comes from all that is. Love gets us thru the days one breath at a time. And when you let the love in, there is not so much room for the pain.

The words below go well with an Angel Hug:

When tomorrow starts without me
and I am not here to see…
If the sun should rise and find your
eyes filled with tears for me.
I wish so much you wouldn't cry
the way you did today…
While thinking many things
we didn't get to say.
I know how much you loved me,
as much as I love you…
And each time you think of me,
I know you'll miss me too.
So when tomorrow starts without me,
don't think we're far apart…
For every time you think of me,
I'm right here in your heart.
~Author Unknown (shortened version)

Amourningmom shares her family's answer to those difficult questions: "How many brothers and sisters do you have?" "How many children do you have?"

Helping with Homework
Posted March 6, 2014
Amourningmom.com

Today's 1st grade homework assignment for one of the twins was about cultural diversity. The questions asked about backgrounds, customs and families. I was helping her with the assignment. We discussed the questions and her answers. "Where are you from?" "Where were you born?" She quickly answered and wrote down, "Atlanta, Georgia." All was going smoothly until we got to the question asking, "How many brothers and sisters do you have?"

I have written before about being asked "How many children do you have?" "How many brothers and sisters do you have?" is the bereaved sibling's version of this question. They are both such common and polite questions but the answers for some of us are so complicated. When people ask me how many children I

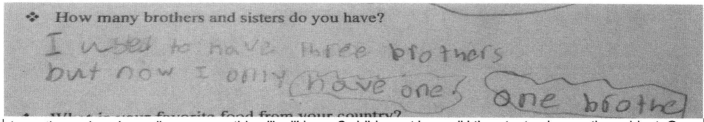

have these days I usually say something like "I have 2 children at home." I then try to change the subject. Or, the other day I caught myself saying "excuse me for a moment" and I left the conversation all together. I always remember Jake and Sawyer but I do not always talk about them. But maybe it does not have to be so difficult.

At first she did not immediately answer the question "How many brothers and sisters do you have?" Instead,

she looked at me thoughtfully and asked, "Mama, how many brothers do I have?" Before I could say anything she said "I know!!" and she began to write . . .

I used to have three brothers but now I only have one. one brother

When she finished writing she went over to her one brother and gave him a hug. And, then I hugged them both.

"Mama whispered softly, time will ease your pain.
Life's about changing, nothing ever stays the same.
And she said, how can I help you to say goodbye?
It's ok to hurt: it's ok to cry.
Come let me hold you, and I will try.
How can I help you to say goodbye."

How Can I Help You Say Goodbye
Patty Loveless

E. Grandparents

Don't forget those people standing beside and behind you.

A mother never "gives up" her baby.

A father never relinquishes his "Little Girl" or his "Son."

Grandparents hurt as much for their own child as for the loss of their grandchild.

Grandparents want to help; they're driven to help by their own anguish. They're watching you.

My dad was there at the right time. He didn't say a word. He just looked at my husband, put his arms around him, and hugged him. My husband broke into tears. I had never seen him cry. It was a real hard cry. It was like he needed the support of a man to understand and hold him without words.
Grief of Grandparents, RTS Bereavement Services

Sometimes, they just don't know how to help.

They often feel helpless themselves. They're forced to acknowledge the loss of their dreams as "grandparents." At the same time, they want to comfort you.

Sometimes they get it right.

When your kids are little you do everything for them. When they grow up and something like this happens, you'd like to do something, but there isn't a lot you can do. You just let them know you feel sorry for them and you are hurting. It isn't like when they were small and hurt their knee. You can kiss it and bandage it up and it's all better in their world. Things like this, you can't.
Grief of Grandparents, RTS Bereavement Services

Sometimes they get it wrong.

"Maybe you shouldn't have been working so hard."

"I knew all that running while you were pregnant wasn't good for the baby."

"I told you you weren't eating right or taking care of yourself. "

If they get it wrong, remember they are hurting too. Sometimes they know how to handle their grief. Sometimes they don't. That doesn't mean they don't want to help or that they don't love your lost child - or you. Listen to Lori Ennis address the pain inflicted by those who just don't understand as she explains "the power of grace."

The Power of Grace...
By Lori Ennis December 6, 2013
Stillstandingmag.com

I have been feeling very sorry for myself lately. Matthew would have blown out four birthday candles last week, and on a day this country designated to give thanks, while I without question was filled with gratitude, I was also missing my little boy terribly. There's never a birthday that's not going to sting, but there's something about it falling on the day we are to be most thankful that really, really, stung.

The next day stung; it was the day he died. Gut-wrenching remembrance.

Yesterday, though. Yesterday was tough. Four years ago, yesterday, I buried my son.

There's something about time. It has a way of erasing things. Sometimes, that's a good thing. You don't want to remember. It hurts your soul too much. But other times? You are desperate to remember. Yesterday, I was desperate to remember. When Matthew died, I was grateful for the chemical reaction of shock in my body. Like many who suffer the loss of a child, I found myself near catatonic. I remember watching things, but not being part of them. I sat in my brown chair or on the sofa, barely moving and listlessly staring. I don't think I spoke much and I'm pretty sure I worried people around me as I held Matthew's blanket, often on my shoulder, patting it, as I would have patted him had he been in my arms.

I don't remember much else. The days and weeks after his death were a blur;...

I wish I'd been in a better state of mind and had paid more attention. I wish I'd picked out pallbearers (thankfully, men at our church stepped in when needed); I wish I asked someone to take pictures. I wish I'd video recorded it. At the time, those ideas seemed morbid, but now, four years later, I find myself desperate to know any detail about his funeral. I can't, and my heart aches in a way that I don't feel it has in a very long time.

I say all of this because I feel it is important to ask people for some grace, especially during the holidays.

You may be thinking of what holiday gifts you need to buy . .. or how awesome a snow day would be but somewhere, some mother is thinking about how she'll never be able to step in a classroom again and that the two feet of snow everyone thinks is so beautiful will forever remind a mother of the worst days of her life. At this time of year, people are hustling and bustling and enjoying the festivities of the season, while others are flashing back to tubes and wires on their newborn. Funerals. Caskets. . .

Some who don't understand why that mother 'just can't be grateful for what she has now' may not realize that the mother will NEVER be able to act like she's never stood in front of the coffin her brand new baby was nearly too long to fit in, but that DOESN'T mean she's not grateful for her blessings in life.

Trust me, gratitude always wins.

But grace…Grace is so healing to a soul. Believe this: Somewhere, someone has said something, unintentionally, that's made a mother or father cringe and writhe inside in emotional pain—but that mother or father gracefully told her or himself it wasn't meant…that they couldn't possible know what it felt like to have their biggest dream in life stolen ruthlessly. They couldn't possibly understand how he or she has been left a scarred, different person forever. They couldn't possibly know or even come close to imagining it, or understand how their lack of understanding or insensitivity hurt. Still, a grief-stricken mother or father gave them grace.

Grace. We, as those who have lost children and in an effort to maintain relationships our fragile hearts cling to, give grace to those people. We give it in spades, and we give it far more often than it is given back.

Give it back! I beg.

Give.it.back.

You just don't know how hard it is to keep the smile on.

Especially during the most wonderful time of the year.

If Grandparents get it right, honor their love. If they don't, honor their love.

Don't be afraid to tell them what you need. If you need groceries, if you need housecleaning, if you need a hug and an excuse to leave a family gathering early, tell them. They want to help. They'll help you find a way.

If you tell them, it will be OK to not be OK. Just tell them you will be OK someday. That's what they need.

Also remember - your parents may be pouring out their strength to you, but they are also dealing with their own loss and uncertainty.

They are facing many of the same social and emotional issues you are dealing with. What do they say to their friends about their lost dreams and the lost future with their grandchild? What are their friends saying to them? The awkwardness you feel with your friends is also reflected in your parents' friends. What do you say to a grandparent who has lost that dream? Do you pull away or do you stay and comfort?

As a grandparent who has lost her dream of a future, how does she answer that inevitable question - "Do you have any grandchildren?"

As much as your parents are helping you, you may need to help them.

We sat there night after night with them but what we did with them was just offer physical comforts. We listened quietly and just poured out our strength to them.

Grief of Grandparents. RTS Bereavement Services

F. Friends

Finally, there are all the people around you.

Sometimes friends are strange and wonderful creatures. You discover they have your back in any situation. You find them, waiting for you, supporting you in whatever happens. As Mommadale says, "You know they are true friends when they hold your son and their heart breaks..."

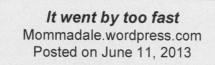

It went by too fast
Mommadale.wordpress.com
Posted on June 11, 2013

... Asher also did the head rearing thing with Justin like he had done with me, and it was probably 20 minutes after we removed him from the ventilator. We were amazed he was still with us, as they didn't think he would breathe very long at all without it. Nope, our baby boy was ONE TOUGH GUY. He is a Martindale- he is stubborn, hard working and doesn't give up without a fight. Since he was still with us, I invited our small group to come inside the curtain with us. My heart was heavy but having this group of people around us, who had began this journey with us, hand in hand, just felt right. It was like each of us were coming full circle in this experience. I was worried that they wouldn't want to be that close to us, watching our son slowly let go but each one of them didn't hesitate. It was a very PERSONAL moment for Justin and I and they all felt honored to stand next to us as Asher left this world. They each took a turn holding him, and that touched my heart. I looked at their faces as they held our little boy, hugging him so tight, with his little arms and legs poking out of their grip. You know they are true friends when they hold your son and their heart breaks just as much as yours when they say goodbye to him.

Sometimes, as in Thelittlegreenfamily, they do something so special and unexpected that it becomes "a top three moment for me in my life."

Day Five: Hallie Lynn Green
(This is Chris. Katie will resume writing soon.)
thelittlegreenfamily.blogspot.com
Posted on December 23, 2011

I can't write a word until I thank all of you who have sent gifts to our house, texted, wrote on the Hope For Hallie Face- book wall, brought meals, and most importantly... prayed for our family and Hallie.

I've got to be honest, when I first saw the signs and hashtags labeled "Hope for Hallie," I was a little nervous. I guess I wanted to make sure people knew what to hope for. The prayers for a miracle of full recovery in Hallie's health have been a braver prayer than I honestly was willing to pray. Probably out of the fear that God might not "fix" her. I also didn't want to assume that Hallie's health was the indicator of God's goodness to us. We've seen God's goodness in so many ways, and greatly through each of you. The bottom line is this: please don't hinge your willingness to believe in God on Hallie's survival.

The reality is, she won't.

I want to follow that horrible sentence with this. Hallie's survival was never our "Hope for Hallie." We knew the day we heard the words "Trisomy 13," Hallie's life would be short, and maybe just hours/days if she survived birth. Our "Hope for Hallie" is that people would see life as a gift, and draw near to God. Based on your comments here, and based on the Facebook wall, I would say: mission accomplished. More people know Hallie's name within the last five days than will know my name throughout my entire life. Please don't feel sorry for Hallie...or us.

We will continue to enjoy every moment we are given with Hallie. We're heartbroken. Extremely heartbroken. We cry...probably hourly. God's purpose for Hallie does not exempt us from the pain of losing her. Don't be misled into thinking we're all laughing and celebrating all of the time.

Hallie is perfectly made for us. She has a cleft lip and palette, no eyes, and we're pretty sure she's deaf. But she's still perfect to us. Her soul shines through her.

Finally, I'll leave you with a shot taken last night shortly after we arrived home from the hospital. One of our "Hope for Hallie" participants (and later found out, a close family friend) went to Bass Pro Shop to do some family photos with Santa. She was holding a "Hope for Hallie" sign in the photo. Santa asked about it, and was moved by our story. He wanted to help bring some Christmas cheer to our family. And...at 9pm last night, after working a strenuous, all-day schedule, he drove the 30 miles south to our home to make us smile.

This single act of selflessness and love has got to be a top-three moment for me in my life. I would compare it to the "Move that Bus!" Extreme Home Makeover emotion. Incredible. He came with two elves (thanks Kristin and Lauren), and brought gifts for our girls and us, prayed for our family, and then lead us all in "Silent Night." I'll have a video of the girls' reaction up...well...soon. Santa, thank you for honoring our family in such a sacrificial way. (I see God's love all over this.)

…

Thank you for loving our special daughter.

Sometimes, however, friends become distant, gone, unable to connect. It's not anyone's fault. It just is. Sometimes you'll find friends have no idea what to say. They either say something painful or they don't say anything at all.

At some of the darkest moments in my life, some people I thought of as friends deserted me — some because they care about me and it hurt them to see me in pain; others because I reminded them of their own vulnerability, and that was more than they could handle. But real friends overcame their discomfort and came to sit with me. It they had not words to make me feel better, they sat in silence (much better than saying), "You'll get over it." or "it's not so bad; others have it worse." And I love them for it.
Harold Kushner, Living a Life that Matters

6 Top Things I Don't Want to Hear
Northsidepnl.blogspot.com
Wednesday, February 23, 2013

My Top 6 Ludicrous and Ridiculous Things People Say After Someone Loses a Baby
(my responses in blue)

1. It just wasn't meant to be. *Ok, obviously not, but how would you feel if your child passed away at any age and I said to you that it wasn't meant to be for that child to continue living and to grow older? Puts a bit of a different spin on it, doesn't it?*

2. You just have to know that God has a plan and your loss is all part of it. *The Tsunami in Tailand and all of the other natural disasters that occur in the world are all part of His plan, too, but that doesn't make them hurt any less.*

3. You can have another baby. *(This is one of my favorites!). Well, unfortunately, I am not as fertile as you are with your x number of kids. And when I do get pregnant, things are not very easy for me. Unless you are absolutely certain that I will be successful in not only getting pregnant, but also being able to carry that baby, please do not comment on my fertility. Maybe, I am unable to have any more children or maybe I have chosen not to have any more. VERY personal comment.*

4. You have your own angel now. *I would move heaven and earth for my baby to be here, with me. I wanted her to bury me, not the other way around. That statement may give me peace one day, but today it really does not.*

5. Try to forget this all happened. *I am so terribly afraid of forgetting. I am afraid of forgetting her movement inside of me, her profile, my pregnancy sickness, my delivery. If I could bottle it all up, I would. That time is part of me and my family. She happened. You may need to forget it or ignore what has happened to me, but I will not. Besides, how would you feel if I said that to you after you lost a loved one?*

6. There was probably something wrong anyway, or she could have had alot of problems. *First of all, why would you ever say that? Second of all, why does that matter? The fact that you think that says alot about your parenting style. So, would you love your child any less if he or she was in an accident that left them impaired? Would that child not still be completely worthy of being here? I would have loved my baby no matter what.*

The sad truth is that I could continue my list. The happy truth is that I have gotten to a point where, most of the time, I don't let these types of comments get to me.

Amourningmom offers her friends some helpful advice. Share these ideas with your friends and family so they can be there for you.

Bring soup, be there & other ways to help a bereaved friend
Amourningmom.com
January 26, 2014

In a few different posts I have written about what people have said to Evan and I after Jake and then Sawyer's deaths. There seem to be endless opportunities in life to say the wrong thing. It is hard to put yourself in another person's shoes and separate out your own feelings. We all have different experiences. We start from a variety of places. Who is to judge what is right and what is wrong? All we can do is try our best.

My mom recently sent me an article called The Art of Presence by David Brooks. It is about a family who has suffered enormous tragedy in their lives (including the death of one of their daughters). The family gives very practical advice such as:

Be a builder.

I had not read/heard this analogy before and I like it so, I am going to share:

"Firefighters drop everything and arrive at the moment of crisis. Builders are there for years and years, walking alongside as the victims live out in the world. Very few people are capable of performing both roles."

A few other pieces of advice I have heard about but are also worth sharing (I may have also written about these before . . .):

· Do be there.
· Even if you do not know what to say it does not matter. Just show up.
· Do not compare, ever.
· There is no comparison contest with bereaved parents. Everyone has lost.
· Bring soup.
· Love and compassion are necessities, not luxuries. Without them humanity cannot survive.
· The Dali Lama
· Do not say you will get over it.
· Grief changes over time but in my experience there is no "healing" from the loss of your child.
· Do not say it is all for the best or try to make sense out of it.
· The death of a child is not for the best and there is no making sense of it for any parent.

In "Walk Beside Me and Be My Friend" Nan Zastrow thanks all her friends - "those that walked with me as well as those that walked away."

Grief forces you to see:
Who matters.
Who never did.
Who won't anymore.
And who always will.

Author Unknown

Walk Beside Me and Be My Friend
Opentohope.com
March 12, 2012, by Nan Zastrow

"A real friend is one who walks in when the rest of the world walks out. Don't walk in front of me, I may not follow. Don't walk behind me, I may not lead. Walk beside me and be my friend." Charles Caleb Colton

My life changed gradually after the death of my son, Chad, on April 16, 1993—and so did many of my friends. A while ago, I met a co-worker whose empathy in my early stage of grief was unconditional. I was reminded of his warmth and support; and it still glowed. Then it hit me! What was different about Steve that made him a loyal, comforting friend when so many others during the same period of time disappeared from my life?

Grief has a way of sorting out those who remain "true" friends and those who "ride off into the sunset." I was puzzled by this enigma. I wondered, "Did my relationship with friends and acquaintances change because of my profound grief that was uncomfortable for them or was it something more than that?"

Why is it that some relationships break down or end after the death of a loved one? Through a personal story, I was able to figure it out.

For many years, my co-worker and our spouses enjoyed social activities together. When Chad died, this couple came to the funeral; but then, I didn't hear from them for over a year. One day my friend called and apologized for ignoring me. She asked if the four of us could get together for dinner.

Halfway through the meal, they started talking about the sporting events in their sons' lives. I said, "I remember when Chad played sports. It seemed we were always ….." Immediately, a silence came over the table. The evening ended abruptly, and we haven't seen them socially since. I felt guilty for bringing up my son's name!

Grief has taught me many lessons. One I learned was: not everyone who was your friend before your loved one's death will be your friend during and after your grief and mourning.

I surmised that my friends changed because they didn't know how to deal with their own feelings about grief and loss. Additionally, they didn't know how to deal with the emotions I was then expressing. I felt confident that this was all there was too it. . . until now. Above and beyond these valid assumptions there was something more.

An even greater reason for the disintegration of relationships was the fact that as I changed— I grew! And, I grew in a different direction—away from them. This isn't a "bad" thing. But I was struck by the significance of my initial reaction that my friends didn't know how to be part of my grief—how to be my friend when I needed them most. I felt betrayed. Through an unstated mutual agreement, we casually drifted apart. They were no longer able to meet my personal needs, and I was destined to "grow" from my experience.

Being a companion in grief is a learned experience for some. It requires taking cues from the bereaved that need to hear the name of their loved one, tell their story, and talk about their experience. . . .

Next to my husband, my sister, Sally, has been my true friend. She admitted often that she couldn't imagine what I was going through. Initially, like others, she believed my pain would heal best if I put my loss behind me, moved on, and forgot about my pain. After a period of time, she realized it wasn't that easy.

Once, I told her my story about two eagles flying over our country home on the anniversary of Chad and Jenny's death. I was sure it was a symbolic message, and it gave me peace. One day, months later, she told me, "Today, I saw two eagles soaring together. I thought of Chad and Jenny." Now that's a friend that was in tune to my needs, listened to my grief, and grew with me! Those friendships lost during grief or gained during grief were critical to my personal spiritual growth. People come in to our lives for different reasons. . . (Remember the story: for a reason, a season, or a lifetime!) Savor every friendship for what it means to you at the time; and you'll be able to accept the few that abandon you when you felt you needed them the most. When a friendship changes, allow yourself to let go of that relationship. You are not responsible for its disintegration. There's a new friend waiting to step into your life.

In my early days of grief, I found a poster that hung in my office and it still applies today.

Who knows the joys that lie ahead
The secret smiles I'll find,
The friends I'll meet
The memories sweet,
The cares I'll leave behind.
Who knows the beauty of the days, I've never seen before.
My only wish for life is this
The courage to explore.
(author unknown)

My husband, my sister, and my friend Steve were genuine friends during grief that met all the criteria. They were willing to walk beside me during the darkest moments and encourage me to find the meaning in my grief experience. Looking back now, I'm grateful for all my friends—those that walked with me and those that walked away. In each circumstance, they gave me the freedom to grow!

Sometimes all you have to do is let friends know it's OK to talk about what happened.

The mention of my child's name **May** *bring tears to my eyes, but it never fails to bring* **Music** *to my ears. If you are truly my friend, let me hear the beautiful music of his name. It soothes my broken heart and sings to my soul. Author Unknown*

Sometimes that's not enough.
You've changed. Relationships change. It's hard.

Ah, I smiled. I'm not really here to keep you from freaking out. I'm here to be with you while you freak out, or grieve or laugh or suffer or sing. It is a ministry of presence. It is showing up with a loving heart Kate Braestrup, Here if You Need Me; A True Story

This is part of life, part of the growth and change that is the basis of "you." If old acquaintances drift away, try to accept and understand, and then look for those who matter - those who understand the enormity of what has happened to you - or if they don't understand, accept.

They are there. Look.

Part 2: **Honor Your Child**

One Little Candle

I lit a candle tonight, in honor of you.
Remembering your life, and all the times we'd been through.
Such a small little light the candle made until I realized
How much in darkness it lit the way.
All the tears I've cried in all my grief and pain
What a garden they grew;
Watered with human rain.
I sometimes can't see beyond the moment,
In hopeless despair
But then your memory sustains me,
In heartaches repair.
I can't wait for the tomorrow,
When my sorrows ease.
Until then, I'll light this candle,
And let my memories run free.

Sheila Simmons

There are no limits to the ways you can honor the life and death of your child. Whatever you can imagine, you can do.

There is something at the core of our shared human condition that infuses art. Art outlives people…art transcends the everyday experience of living as it transcends time. This kind of art is not merely decorative. It is a mix of ritual and craft, a gesture that means more than an artwork to adorn a pleasant room. It might even be seen as a kind of "holy rite".
Katherine Reif-Canas, opentohope.com

Paint a picture. Write a song, a poem, a blog - or a book. Write a letter to him. Plant a tree. Have jewelry made with her birthstone. Donate time or money to a favorite charity in his name. Northsidepnl.blogspot, Amourningmom, and Littlewingedones describe ways they honor their children:

The Wisdom of Pooh
Northsidepnl.blogspot.com
Wednesday, July 13, 2013

If you have read this blog for a while, you may know that I love the beach. I am most definitely a summer girl. No mountains for me....it is the beach that makes me happy. You know also, too, that since I lost my baby daughter, it is our big summer beach trip to Longboat Key that makes me really miss her the most. Strangely, for me, it is not Christ- mas or Mother's Day. It is the summer family trip and Halloween (I know that is odd, but I can't help it) that affect me the most. Maybe because during that trip, my family spends so much time together. It, for us, is our time to not think about anything but family, take our family beach pictures, spend time with cousins, etc, etc. It makes me remember that there is a little girl missing. A little girl who would be 3 and a half, who may or may not like the ocean, who would probably love flying a kite, who would be so pooped by the end of the day that her daddy and I would put her to bed early. A little girl with pink cheeks and probably blonde hair. Oh, I miss that girl! Which confuses me so much....how do you miss what you don't know? I guess

I miss knowing her. I have missed it all. And sometimes that hits me like a freight train.

It is crazy, though, that for the past couple of years, when I start to get really down about missing her on our trip, I see something that just takes my breath away. One year it was a school of about 10 dolphins that put on a show right in front of me. Last year, it was the manatee that came and drank right from a water hose I was holding on a dock! Well, this year, just as I was about to start crying, I laid my head on my knees and looked to the left and this is what I saw....

Isn't that gorgeous?! The crazy part is that it had not rained yet. It was cloudy, but no rain. I just love that rainbow right over my favorite ocean. Such a precious message from my sweet girl. Just reminding me that she was right there with us.

A very dear person made some memory boxes for our office recently. They are amazing. She is so creative and took so much time making them and really poured her heart into them. She is another mom who is missing her baby.

One of her boxes had the following quote from the A.A. Milne Winnie the Pooh series:

"If ever there is tomorrow when we're not together... there is something you must always remember. You are braver than you believe, stronger than you seem, and smarter than you think. But the most important thing is, even if we're apart... I'll always be with you."
— A.A. Milne

I needed to read that. I hope she knows how much that touched me and will touch the family who reads it. There is so much truth and wisdom in that statement.

So, I am now obsessed with what I call "Pooh Wisdom". I have read some of the most loved quotes from A.A. Milne. What incredible works of literature! I have never noticed before, but most of Pooh's best-loved quotes speak right to your soul.

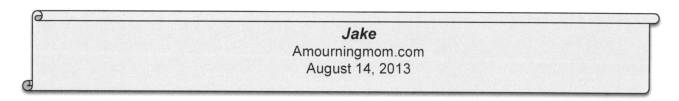

So, here is to rainbows on the beach. And a honey bear named Pooh and all of his sidekicks. And to all of you who are right there with me, missing the part of you that is no longer here. We are all in this together, one small step at a time.

Jake
Amourningmom.com
August 14, 2013

Dear Jake, Today you would/should have been 8. You are not. I am still so very thankful that I got to meet you. I just wish we could have kept you for longer. Below are the words that your dad wrote to you 8 years ago. They are just as true today.

We love you Jake.

You are our sunshine.

You are such a courageous and strong fighter, and we are so proud of you.

Jake, you are a miracle, and we thank you for choosing us to be your parents.

You are so wise for someone so young and so small. You knew when you had to come into this world Jake, and you knew when you had to leave us to be in a better place.

You are and were the perfect son for us.

Jake, please know that we felt all the love you gave to us during your time here.

We are sad that we could only spend such a short time with you, but we are so glad and thankful for every minute of it.

It is amazing how we could come to love you so immediately and so completely even though we were just getting to know each other.

Then again, we feel like we have known you all of our lives, and you will be in our hearts forever and beyond.

Jake, we also know that you are at peace and that you are being watched over by all of our loved ones who also watch over all of us from above.

Thank you, Jake.

Thank you for coming to us.

Thank you for choosing us.

Thank you for loving us and letting us love you with all of our hearts.

We'll see you every night playing up with the moon and the stars.

I miss you every. single. day. Some days are harder than others. I love you.

Write his name in the sand and take a picture or write them in the sky and let the whole world see.

Some families include siblings in these remembrances.

Their names
Littlewingedones.com
POSTED ON DECEMBER 2, 2013 BY EILEEN TULLY

We decorated our Christmas tree yesterday.

It's something I always love to do. The kids get excited going through the boxes and finding their favorite ornaments, selecting just the right spot for each one. And it is fun to watch a new baby see the tree for the very first time. Our Maeve was just weeks old last Christmas, so this year, she is toddling all around, stealing ornaments, and pointing in awe at the lights. Every day is like Christmas for her as she comes out of her room in the morning and sees it again for the first time.

Last year, we made a few switches. We're making new family traditions and watching the evolution of what will be the Tully Family Christmas. We went from white lights to multicolored ones. We went from an angel on top to a star. Our children voiced their preferences and we were happy to oblige them.

Except that not all of our kids are here to weigh in. And with the holiday season also comes the reminder that there could be more little Tullys telling us their favorite Christmas things to do. There could be more stockings lined up and more ornaments and more gifts. More giggles and smiles and faces lighting up with the tree. For some of us, our only little ones are missing from our hearts and our homes this year, and we struggle to get through the "most wonderful time of the year" when our hearts are broken and there is a dull ache inside us that makes us want to curl up in a ball and not get out of bed.

So if someone you love is missing their little one this year, can I just make a recommendation for the greatest gift you can give them? It won't cost much. It could cost nothing. But it will be something they will love and remember you fondly for.

The gift of using their baby's name.

Say it out loud.

Include it on a Christmas card. "Remembering ___ with you this Christmas."

Give an ornament that has it on there.

Maybe a piece of jewelry with it engraved in beautiful letters.

ANYTHING.

I promise they will treasure it.

Copyright 2013 Eileen Tully. Used with permission from the author.

Do Not Stand at My Grave and Weep

Do not stand at my grave and weep,
I am not there, I do not sleep.
I am in a thousand winds that blow,
I am the softly falling snow.
I am the gentle showers of rain,
I am the fields of ripening grain.
I am in the morning hush,
I am in the graceful rush
Of beautiful birds in circling flight,
I am the star shine of the night,
I am in the flowers that bloom,
I am in a quiet room.
I am in the birds that sing,
I am in each lovely thing.
Do not stand at my grave and cry,
I am not there. I do not die.

Mary Elizabeth Frye

Treasure the small things that belong to her - a blanket, a teddy bear. They are powerful memories of a life. Find creative ways to memorialize and remember him. Amourningmom bought a star:

Second star
Amourningmom.com
February 18, 2014

When Jake died the hospital gave us a packet of information to take home. I remember trying to read it through my tears and being unable to make out most of the words. When I got to the page on "Ways to Honor Your Child" I got a tissue, wiped my eyes and read. One of the ways was to name a star. Before I knew it I was on the phone buying a star for Jake:

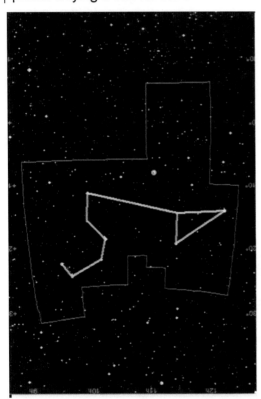

The star date is his birthday and it is in the constellation of Leo (Jake's zodiac sign). We have the star certificate with all of Jake's other belongings. I think before now the only other person I told that I bought a star was Evan. Buying the star made me feel a bit better for the moment. It was something I could do for Jake. Funny how time changes some things. . .

After Sawyer died I did not buy a star. The thought of buying another star did not make me feel better. Recently, I came across Jake's star certificate and decided that I did want a star for Sawyer after all.

I tried to order it online and then finally called. I wanted Sawyer's star date to be his birthday, just like Jake's. The star registry only goes back 2 years - which meant 2012, 2013 or this year. There is no 2009 option. I chose this year - for Sawyer's 5th birthday.

Sibling rivalry is an issue at times in our house with the twins. I will never know if Sawyer would be unhappy that Jake had a star and he did not but the second star bought to avoid any worries. It made me feel a bit better and it was something I could do for Sawyer.

If she is fighting to live or has already died,
write a letter that expresses your love and your pride.

Whatever you choose to do anything you choose to do - is OK. It's yours.

There is no "right" or "wrong" way to grieve. There is no "right" or "wrong" way to honor. And, as Mommadale says, "He is gone only for a moment but he will never be a stranger. . ."

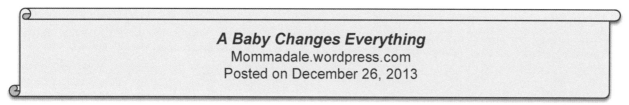

A Baby Changes Everything
Mommadale.wordpress.com
Posted on December 26, 2013

Well, we are hoping and praying for another baby. It's been 7 months ago today that our little man entered our lives and we want to hold and love another just as we do Asher. I told Justin yesterday that when we have more kids, I want one of the traditions on Christmas to be them filling Asher's stocking. I want them to know him, to talk to him, to have pictures of him in their room. He is gone only for a moment but he will never be a stranger to any of our future children.

Part 3: **Life After Loss**

Believe it or not, life goes on.

The hardest thing that I've ever had to hear was that my child died. The hardest thing that I've ever done is to live every day since that moment.
Amourningmom.com

The world goes on. The seasons change. Weeks, months, and years pass. Grief changes, slowly, and everyone has a personal timeline.

You will never forget. Your grief will never go away, but somehow it will become easier to bear. It will be easier to move forward.

There will be triggers - Your Due Date, Mother's or Father's Day, Christmas, Birthdays, the day they were born or died. Expect those times to be stressful and take extra care to be kind to yourself, your partner, your other children, and your family.

Remember, it's always OK to not be OK. Amourningmom says, "I just need to realize that is all part of life and hold on."

Control & Clean Clothes
Amourningmom.com
September 26, 2013

I wish life could be a bit more like laundry. You put the dirty clothes in the washing machine, add detergent and wait. After the clothes are clean put them into the dryer. Wait. Fold.

Okay, it is not always so seamless. I have turned a few white loads pink. I will also confess that I have washed more than one diaper. It is pretty messy. However, after shaking out the clothes and repeating the wash and dry cycles everything was once again clean.

Before 2005 there were plenty of situations out of my control but Jake's diagnosis put them all into perspective for me. I did what I thought were the right steps. I gave birth to Jake at 26 weeks anyway. He lived for 2 weeks but I could not do a thing to prevent his death.

At the time I thought that I could protect any potential future children if they were not premature. I could be in control if I could just keep them out of the NICU. Sawyer's death let me know loud and clear that I was wrong about that too.

Lately, life seems more out of control than I would like. I just need to realize that is all part of life and hold on. I think I will go switch the laundry into the dryer.

Ask family to help with awkward moments or invitations. Be honest and open about your feelings and fears. You may find yourself re-experiencing mood swings and emotions you felt at the time of your loss. That's OK. Remember what you did to cope then and try to put some of those strategies into place again - for a brief time or as long as you need.

Remember. It's OK to be happy.

Allowing yourself to laugh and love doesn't mean you're not honoring her. It means you're human and you're working towards healing with love. You will begin to enjoy the beauty of the world again. It just takes time.

Some say holding on is what makes you strong, but sometimes it takes much more strength to just let go and move on.

Author Unknown

Dancing in the Rain
Northsidepnl.blogspot.com
Wednesday April 3, 2014

I was reminded the other day of one of my favorite quotes. It is actually the quote at the top of this blog...."Life is not about surviving the storm....it is about learning to dance in the rain." It is an anonymous quote that I read years ago. I have always liked it. It always made me think of strength in hard times. This quote took on a completely new meaning for me after my daughter's stillbirth.

I spent a lot of time just getting by. In the first days, I thought I was doing really well if I got up and took a shower. I made myself do that. After the first 2 or 3 weeks, I made a deal with myself....

I decided that I could do anything for 15 minutes each day. My "anything", the thing I dreaded most was being "normal" for 15 minutes. That meant I would not be sad for 15 minutes. Not let my sadness bring me down for a whole 15 minutes. I could do it. Fifteen minutes and then, I could go back to being sad. As long as I knew I could go back to bed if I wanted or spend the afternoon crying if I wanted, I could handle the 15 minutes.

I know it may sound completely crazy, but it gave me something to focus on. A goal for the day. Sometimes, my fifteen minutes involved reading a fun magazine or a book that made me laugh. Sometimes it meant catching up on my favorite soap (which is Young and the Restless, BTW :)) I watched the clock most of the time and when the time was up, I went back to being sad. I don't know if this makes sense, but I needed the time of being sad. I needed to feel what I was feeling. I needed to have that time with my baby, thinking of her and mourning her. There were days when
I couldn't wait for the 15 minutes to be over, so I could get back to reality. I needed to stand in the storm, so to speak. To be knocked over by the hurricane force winds that kept pounding me. I was in survival mode and I needed to survive the storm that was my loss.

An interesting thing happened. I don't even know when it did, but it happened. It was so gradual that I never even noticed. I stopped watching the clock. I stopped counting the 15 minutes. I don't even know when I noticed that I had begun spending more time each day doing something happy. Of course, then I felt guilty that I had been happy. But I shouldn't have. I guess you can say that I was learning to dance again. I just didn't know it.

Even though the storm of that awful time had passed, nothing was the same. Nothing ever will be the same. So, I had find my way of being normal again. Many people call it the "new normal". I guess you can say it is like dancing in the rain.

I read something the other day that a friend posted on her Facebook page. She was talking about rainbows and how you can't see a rainbow unless you have had the rain and the sun. I love what she wrote. It is so very true. My daughter has brought me so much sunshine. Her life and death have taught me so much about myself. If it weren't for her, I don't know that I would be the person I am. She shapes me everyday. She has taught me so much about dancing in the rain.

There comes a time in life, after something gut wrenching and horrible has happened, that you have to make some decisions. Are you going to sink in the horrible hole that is grief or are you going to swim in the vast ocean that is life? Are you going to let the storm knock you down or are you going to get out there and dance right in that rain?

I have chosen to dance and it is a wonderful dance filled with hope and laughter and gratitude, and yes, sadness. This dance is mine and my daughter's...it is what we are doing together.

I hope you learn to dance again, too, and that the dance is precious and sweet and honors your baby the way that you want it to.

It's also OK to move forward. Fathersgrievinginfantloss and Mommadale begin to put this into perspective.

Intimacy & Subsequent Pregnancy – When?
Fathersgrievinginfantloss.blogspot.com

Whenever I bring this topic up while speaking to a group, there are always a few red faces and eyes darting to the floor. Frankly, that's what makes it such an important point to discuss. Many of us find it hard to express our sexual needs, desires, fears, and insecurities under the best of circumstances. When you add grief to the mix, it can get really dicey and be a topic we simply want to avoid.

If you are lucky enough to be comfortable talking about this stuff to your partner, you are lucky, and probably will not see what the big deal is. But, if you find this difficult, it can be a real source of problems that can result in adding to feelings of loneliness and isolation.

So -- when is the right time to resume sexual relations? When is the right time to start trying to have another baby? What if one of you wants to try again but the other just isn't sure they want to?

Unfortunately, there are no black and white answers to any of these questions. Like everything, it depends on your situation -- physical condition, emotional state of mind, relationship, and numerous other factors. Often times people will hear that you should wait a minimum of six months to a year before trying again. Depending on the circumstances
and timing of your loss, that makes total sense, and any decision about the physical and emotional risks of another pregnancy should first be discussed with your doctor.

Sometimes the tougher question can be when to resume being intimate? Again, physical considerations are part of that decision, but most of the time this decision "simply" requires communication between you and your partner about your feelings.... Come to think of it, maybe THAT'S why I recall avoiding this topic with my wife.

Seriously, while we definitely felt close emotionally in our need to be held and comforted -- especially when trying to sleep through the night -- neither of us mentioned how we were feeling about sex. When it got to the point that I was feeling like I wanted to, I wondered how I would deal with the guilt of having a moment of pleasure? Those feelings were compounded because I then wondered if it would affect my performance, and that REALLY made me insecure! But, once we were able to talk about it and I realized that we each had our own set of emotions surrounding that moment, we were able to relax and things just happened naturally.

As for another pregnancy, after discussing our situation with our doctor, he felt comfortable supporting us in trying again. Because it had taken us over two years to get pregnant the first time, we decided that we should go for it sooner than later since we were in agreement about wanting more children, if possible. Surprisingly, Monica got pregnant right away, and three months after Kathleen's death, we were expecting another baby. We were very happy, of course, but we had not stopped to think what our timing in starting to try could potentially mean. Our next child was actually due on Kathleen's birthday, and the feelings of deja vu were tremendously stressful for me. I found myself working hard to not get excited because the bliss of pregnancy was gone and it simply became a time to survive. Even all these years later, I have some regrets about what I missed out on during that time in terms of being able to feel the anticipation and excitement of expecting a child.

Keep in mind this is only MY experience. I can definitely tell you that Monica did not feel the same way and her version of this story would be very different from what I just shared.

I guess that really is the point. Don't think that any story you hear suddenly means you know how you're going to feel. These decisions are unique to you and very important to your relationship. No desire or fear is wrong and there is no reason to judge harshly either yourself or your partner. While you may not have previously ever had the need to discuss your sex life with your mate because you were on the same page, know that may not be the case right now. It certainly doesn't mean your marriage is in trouble, but you both should realize the importance of being open and understanding of one another.

Just Keep Swimming
Mommadale.wordpress.com
Posted on June 26, 2013

It's here. June 26, 2013. The day I wrote in our calendar "Baby Martindale due" months ago. The day we put in our Christmas cards that we were expecting a new member of our family. It's the date I started counting down to when we first heard it back in October. Today is the day that brings a lot of mixed emotions. Not only is it Asher's original due date but he would be one month old today. Instead of taking the photo of him wearing a onesie that says "One Month" on it, I am reflecting on what was, what could have been, and what should have been.

I have to be honest, I knew today would be especially difficult. I chose not to go back to work until this day past as I wanted to be able to stay in bed, read books to Asher and just live in the moment with him~100% focused on HIM today. Nothing and no one else. So what did I decide to do this morning? I thought it was fitting to watch a kids movie with him and Asher bear as I drank my coffee. And the movie of choice?? Finding Nemo.

It's funny that yes, it is a children's movie but I kept catching one liners and quotes that spoke right to me, and to this situation I find myself in today. For instance, when Marlin is talking to the sea turtle Crush, he asks him "How do you know when it is time to let go?" to which Crush responds, " when they know, YOU'LL know". That made me flashback to when we took Asher off the ventilator. He stayed with us longer than any of us thought he would, as I guess he wasn't quite ready. He needed some snuggle time with Mommy and Daddy~enough to last him and us a lifetime. I always wonder when I lose loved ones, when they are on the cusp of death, what it is like. Are there angels right there, calmly telling them everything will be okay? Are they telling them that when they are ready, to follow them? I don't know but I can only assume that it's like Crush said, when they know, we'll know.

And then there is the part of the movie where Dory and Marlin find themselves in the whale's mouth, about to be eaten. Dory is telling Marlin to let go and swim to the back of the throat so they can get outta there. Marlin asks Dory, " How do you know nothing bad is going to happen?" to which she calmly, and without fear or hesitation, responds " I don't". Wow. A very simple statement but oh so true. My husband and I are living this right now in regards to our next steps. Do we adopt and take the risk of the birth mother changing her mind? Do we try for another baby of our own and risk reliving this situation all over again? That's the pickle of it all. We DON'T know nothing bad is going to happen. It's a risk. EVERYTHING in life is a risk.

I'll Lend You a Child

"I'll lend you for a little time a child of mine, he said."
For you to love - while he lives,
And mourn for when he's dead.
It may be six or seven years,
Or twenty-two or three, but will you,
Till I call him back, take care of him for me?
He'll bring his smiles to gladden you,
And should this stay be brief,
You'll have his lovely memories as solace for your grief.
I cannot promise he will stay,
Since all from earth return.
But there are lessons taught down there
I want this child to learn.
I've looked this world over
In search for teachers true.
And from the throngs that crowd life's lanes,
I have selected you.
Now will you give him all your love,
Nor count the labor vain,
Nor hate me when I come
To call to take him back again?"
I fancied that I heard them say,
"Dear Lord, Thy will be done,
For all the joy Thy child shall bring,
The risk of grief we'll run.
We'll shelter him with tenderness;
We'll love him while we may.
And for the happiness we've known
Forever grateful stay.
But should the angels call for him
Much sooner than we've planned.
We'll brave the bitter grief that comes
And try to understand.

Edgar Guest

And then there is the light that appears "after darkness and clouds."

Rainbow Baby is Coming...Tomorrow!!!
Thelittlegreenfamily.blogspot.com

We are welcoming a new, beautiful, precious baby to our family tomorrow.

Mystery Baby or Green Baby #4 is also known as a "Rainbow Baby."

Rainbow Babies are known as babies born to a family after the loss of a child. It's something that is "beautiful and full of light and has appeared after darkness and clouds."

I am beyond excited to meet this sweet face that has been bouncing around for 39 weeks. And these two little girls have been counting down the days with me for quite a while, practicing changing diapers and getting pumped about being big sisters.

Words can't really explain my excitement. God is so good. We are blessed!

DESIDERATA

*Go placidly amid the noise and haste, and
remember what peace there may be in
silence.*

*As far as possible, without surrender,
Be on good terms with all persons.
Speak your truth quietly and clearly;
And listen to others,
even to the dull and the ignorant;
they too have their story.*

*Avoid loud and aggressive persons;
They are vexatious to the spirit.
If you compare yourself with others,
You may become vain or bitter,
For always there will be greater and lesser
persons than yourself.*

*Enjoy your achievements as well as your plans.
Keep interested in your own career,
however humble;
It is a real possession in the changing fortunes
of time.*

*Exercise caution in your business affairs,
For the world is full of trickery.
But let this not blind you to what virtue
there is;
Many persons strive for high ideals,
And everywhere life is full of heroism.*

*Be yourself.
Especially, do not feign affection.
Neither be cynical about love;
For in the face of all aridity and disenchantment,
it is perennial as the grass.*

*Take kindly the counsel of the years,
Gracefully surrendering the things of youth.
Nurture strength of spirit to shield you in sudden
misfortune.
But do not distress yourself with dark imaginings.
Many fears are born of fatigue and loneliness.*

*Beyond a wholesome discipline,
Be gentle with yourself.
You are a child of the universe
No less than the trees and the stars;
You have a right to be here.
And whether or not it is clear to you,
No doubt the universe is unfolding as it should.
Therefore be at peace with God,
Whatever you conceive Him to be,
And whatever your labors and aspirations,
In the noisy confusion of life, keep peace in
your soul.*

*With all its sham, drudgery and broken dreams,
It is still a beautiful world.*

Be cheerful.

Strive to be happy.

Max Ehrmann

Appendix

Following are a collection of readings, articles, and resources we hope you will find helpful. There are many resources available on-line and in print, and it may take you some time to find authors or themes with whom you connect. Keep on trying.

Here, our goal is to help you get started.   Find your own voice in this community. Explore and follow some of the bloggers and authors referenced in this book. They can help. Research and look to local support groups, friends, pastors, family.   Keep looking.

What Makes a Mother?
Northsidepnl.blogspot.com
Wednesday May 8, 2014

I have been thinking a lot about Mother's Day this week, with it coming up on Sunday. I know most moms in the baby- loss community have probably been thinking about it too. Maybe dreading it, maybe not. Either way, it is in the minds of many mothers.

My stillborn daughter did not make me a mother. Her older sister has that distinction. What she did make me is a better mother, or so I hope. She taught me what it means to really BE a mother. Ironic, because I never brought her home. I never gave her baths at night and never read Goodnight Moon to her. I have never had to put band aids on her scraped up knees or mend her broken heart. I have never been able to paint her fingernails pink or enroll her in ballet. When I think of the things I would have done with her, as her mother, the part of my heart that stays forever broken starts to hurt.

She came into my life so quickly and left much too soon. And in that short, short time, she changed me. She taught me so much more about being a mother than I could have learned from anyone else. The lessons she taught aren't found in parenting books. You see, they could never do justice to this. There is no book that tells you how to live without your baby. How to wake up every day and remember that she is not here. How to handle seeing 4 year old little girls, knowing that for the rest of the day, you will remember your little girl who would be 4. The books don't tell you how to honor that baby and her short life. They certainly don't make mention of the fact that many of the world's best mothers are mothering babies that they can't hold.

Those lessons I have learned from her. If it weren't for her, I don't know if I would look at the rainbows and the tulips in the backyard, or the white butterflies the same way. I don't know if I would hug my children, her siblings, as tightly as I do. She taught me that love is fierce. And love is stronger than death. And love doesn't go away. She showed me the lengths that I would go to in order to keep her alive in everyone's hearts and minds. I am her mother and it is up to me to remember her and honor her. I do that everyday in the ways that I treat others and the ways that I love her daddy and siblings and grandparents.

I am her mother and she is my daughter. I am so very proud of that fact and will be thinking of her and her impact on me, especially this Sunday. Much peace to all of you this weekend.

Dear Stuck,

Don't listen to those people who suggest you should be "over" your daughter's death by now. The people who squawk the loudest about such things have almost never had to get over anything. Or at least not anything that was genuinely. . . .soul-crushingly life altering. Some of those people believe they're being helpful by minimizing your pain. Others are scared of the intensity of your loss and so they use their words to push your grief away. Many of those people love you and are worthy of your love, but they are not the people who will be helpful to you when it comes to healing the pain of your daughter's death.

They live on Planet Earth. You live on Planet My Baby Died.

It seems to me you feel like you're all alone there. You aren't . . .

This is how you get unstuck, Stuck. You reach. Not so you can walk away from the daughter you loved, but so you can live the life that is yours - the one that includes the sad loss of your daughter, but is not arrested by it. The one that eventually leads you to a place in which you not only grieve her, but also feel lucky to have had the privilege of loving her. That place of true healing is a fierce place. It's a giant place. It's a place of monstrous beauty and endless dark and glimmering light. And you have to work really, really, really hard to get there, but you can do it. You're a woman who can travel that far. I know it. Your ability to get there is evident to me in every word of your bright shining grief star of a letter. . . .

You will never stop loving your daughter. You will never forget her. You will always know her name. But she will always be dead. Nobody can intervene and make that right and nobody will. Nobody can take it back with silence or push it away with words. Nobody will protect you from your suffering. You can't cry it away or eat it away or stare it away or walk it away or punch it away or even therapy it away. It's just there and you have to survive it. You have to endure it. You have to live through it and love it and move on and be better for it and run as far as you can in the direction of your best and happiest dreams across the bridge that was built by your own desire to heal. Therapists and friends and other people who live on Planet My Baby Died can help you along the way, but the healing - the genuine healing, the actual real deal down-on-your-knees-in-the-mud change - is entirely and absolutely up to you.

Tiny Beautiful Things by Cheryl Strayed

The Mourner's Bill of Rights

Alan D. Wolfelt, Ph.D. Copyright 2007-2013, Center for Loss and Life Transition

You have to experience your own unique grief

No one else will grieve in exactly the same way you do. So, when you turn to others for help, don't allow them to tell what you should or should not be feeling.

You have the right to talk about your grief

Talking about your grief will help you heal. Seek out others who will allow you to talk as much as you want, as often as you want, about your grief. If at times you don't feel like talking, you also have the right to be silent.

You have the right to feel a multitude of emotions

Confusion, disorientation, fear, guilt and relief are just a few of the emotions you might feel as part of your grief journey. Others may try to tell you that feeling angry, for example, is wrong, Don't take these judgmental responses to heart. Instead, find listeners who will accept your feelings without condition.

You have the right to be tolerant of your physical and emotional limits

Your feelings of loss and sadness will probably leave you feeling fatigued. Respect what your body and mind are telling you. Get daily rest. Eat balanced meals. And don't allow others to push you into doing things you don't feel ready to do.

You have the right to experience "griefbursts"

Sometimes, out of nowhere, a powerful surge of grief may overcome you. This can be frightening, but is normal and natural. Find someone who understands and will let you talk it out.

You have the right to make use of ritual

The funeral ritual does more than acknowledge the death of someone loved. It helps provide you with the support of caring people. More importantly, the funeral is a way for you to mourn. If others tell you the funeral or other healing rituals such as these are silly or unnecessary, don't listen.

You have the right to embrace your spirituality

If faith is a part of your life, express it in ways that seem appropriate to you. Allow yourself to be around people who understand and support your religious beliefs. If you feel angry at God, find someone to talk with who won't be critical of your feelings of hurt and abandonment.

You have the right to search for meaning

You may find yourself asking, "Why did he or she die? Why this way? Why now?" Some of your questions may have answers, but some may not. And watch out for the clichéd responses some people may give you. Comments like, "It was God's will" or "Think of what you have to be thankful for" are not helpful and you do not have to accept them.

You have the right to treasure your memories

Memories are one of the best legacies that exist after the death of someone loved. You will always remember. Instead of ignoring your memories, find others with whom you can share them.

You have the right to move toward your grief and heal

Reconciling your grief will not happen quickly. Remember, grief is a process, not an event. Be patient and tolerant with yourself and avoid people who are impatient and intolerant with you. Neither you nor those around you must forget that the death of someone loved changes your life forever.

Recommended Articles

First postpartum dr's visit after loss
http://facesofloss.com/real-advice/first-postpartum-drs-visit-after-losing-your-baby

The following tips and advice were submitted by real women when asked what they wish someone would have told them before going to their first postpartum appointment after losing their baby. The raw, honest truth about what it's like. If you have advice you'd like to add, please send it to april@facesofloss.com, with 'real advice' in the subject line. Thanks!

- "Ask to be taken to an exam room immediately! I didn't know I could do that and I had to sit in the waiting room amongst all the pregnant moms and newborns. My first postpartum appointment was 5 days after her birth to have my staples removed so I certainly wasn't ready to sit with all the happy moms." - Mary

- "I wasn't prepared for them to not ask me anything related to losing my baby. It was a checkup and that was it. Really strange to me that they didn't bring it up and talk to me about how I was dealing with it." - Ashley

- "Bring along a friend or a loved one. It's not a good experience to go through by yourself." – Josie

- "I was very unprepared for a pregnancy test, I knew that's why I had to give a urine sample and watched them do the test and it came up negative was a huge slap in the face!" - Courtney

- "After my first loss I wasn't prepared for the receptionist to not know what happened and when I walked in she asked me what I had and was looking around for my baby. Then I had to tell her we lost twins right in front of a bunch of other women." - Ashley

- "We took our sweet boy's picture book with us…. (it only helped a little) but I loved it when my dr asked if she could please post his picture on her wall." - Mari

- "The first thing the nurse asked me was "I see you had your son two weeks ago, how is he doing?" - Amanda

- "I wasn't prepared to be asked by the dr. when we were going to start trying again." - Beryl

- "Make an appt first thing in the morning or at the very end of the day, when it may be less busy. You can also call ahead and ask that they take you straight back to an exam room, so you don't have to sit in the waiting room with other pregnant women. I also think you should take a friend or support person with you. We also let our children bake cookies and make thank you notes for the doctors and all the staff that took care of us. It was part of the healing for us." - Chasity

- "Do not expect to necessarily have all of your questions answered about the possibility of trying again. We were just recommended to a high-risk specialist OB-GYN and the appointment was over a month later. Not surprising now that we think about it, but we were really looking forward to having those questions answered at that first appointment." - Jenny

- "My first appointment was 3 days after losing our son, if it wasn't bad enough to be in the office surrounded by happy pregnant women, the front desk receptionist asked me if I was still pregnant! As for the actual visit with my doctor she wanted to know what my plans were, birth control or keep trying. Not what I wanted to talk about. I wish she would have prepared me for my milk coming in. No one told me that was gonna happen or be so painful both physically or emotionally." - Amy"I wish I had asked for more help. The "I can do it myself" attitude was not helpful for my healing or grief. Ask for help, even if you don't want to." -Ida

- "My first appt was a blur for me. My best advice would be to tell your Dr exactly what you are feeling. Ask all questions of what happened and why. Lean on your Dr. He's there to help you get through it the best he can. I told my Dr exactly what I was thinking and feeling. I was a little angry with him and I had to tell him." -Christa

- "When I called to set up my postpartum appointment, before hanging up the receptionist told me "Congrats!" on the arrival of my twins. That caught me off guard. And I did not know I could ask to be taken back to a room right away when I did go in….sitting in the waiting room filled with pregnant women was torture." -Trena

- "I was not prepared for my doctors to call my D&C an abortion. I didn't choose to lose my baby. It was also hard to get an u/s and know there wouldn't be a baby on the screen." -Megan

- "The waiting room was torture. I was also asked what we wanted to do about birth control. I would suggest having a list of questions you are thinking/want to ask. Ex. When will I get my first period? When can we try again?" -Brooke

- "We were asked to about how we were going to pay our bill right away… not at our 6 week check up but 7 days after my c-section when I went to get my stitches out (2 days after my daughter passed away). We were so out of it that we just put it all on a credit card - now we found out that we have a credit because they overcharged us. If I would have been thinking straight I would have told them that I was going to wait until we heard back from the insurance co." -Shanna

- "See if you could be taken to a room other than one you had been seen in during pregnancy. ASK that everyone in the office be informed about your loss before you go in. I was asked by a nurse if I was breastfeeding. Oh also the wall of newborn pictures was horrible. I had to walk right by it. And the birth control subject- my dr. really started pushing Morena, and I wasn't ready to make that decision yet." - Mandy

- "My suggestion is to have a list of things you want to ask. When you make your appointment, ask them to make sure all staff know you have lost your baby/ies. Be up front with the doctor about everything - trying again, your emotions, EVERYTHING! If you don't speak up, they don't know." -Maureen

- "Expect the nurses and staff who may not know what happened to ask "oh hi! Where's the baby?!?" stab right in the gut…" -Kaila

Going Back to Work
http://facesofloss.com/real-advice/going-back-to-work

Going back to work after suffering the loss of a baby can be another daunting task you are facing. We hope that these tips, submitted by real women who have been there, can help you face it with strength and courage.

If you have advice you'd like to add, please send it to april@facesofloss.com, with 'Going Back to Work' in the subject line. Thanks!

- Take all the time you need/can afford to.
  Rushing back to work before you are ready because you feel obligated is not going to be good for anyone.

- I went back after 2 weeks but I think that was too soon. I would say at least a month, give yourselves time to mourn before having to deal with the work force again. - Stacy

- Hubby went back to work after 2 weeks, I was still healing and trying to cope with the loss and didn't go back to work for 3 months…. My advice is take all the time you need! - Ivy

- There's no right or wrong time. Time is needed to get through the physical symptoms and the emotional is ongoing recovery. Keeping busy does help. - Gina

- Do it in your own time…. Never be pushed into it! No one knows the pain you feel. - Tracy

- My husband took 2 full weeks off and still takes a day off here and there. He's just taking it as it comes and doing what feels comfortable. I'm a SAHM so it wasn't something I had to face, just getting back into the daily routine with my daughter. - Sara

- For some people going back is the right thing to do - and if that's you, don't feel bad about it. - Beth

- Take your time. If you can function again with everyday things like shopping, washing, cooking and they aren't scary anymore then maybe you could face work again. - Leanne

- I think most people forget you still have to recover physically…you still just had a baby! I took almost my full maternity leave, 3 months, because grief drains your energy and ability to heal quickly…It was important to me to have time where I didn't have to "hold it together" but got time to just "be" in my grief full time. – Mary

- I took a week and a half off after my loss at 14 weeks. It wasn't enough time. I was emotional, broken, angry and not ready for work. Please, take the time you need to heal, work will find a way to be okay. You need to get better. It was a big regret of mine. - Michelle

If you are able to, go back slowly.

Start back on a Wednesday or Thursday. That way you'll only have a short week to face when you start.

- I would recommend taking it slowly, step by step. Going in for a meeting, then do half-day for a week, perhaps longer. I went back to work 3 months after my loss and am only now getting my energy back 5 months after my loss. - Anna Lísa

- Go slowly…work a few hours at first and let someone in the office know the plan so that if you leave earlier they know why. I went back three weeks after and I feel like it was too soon for me..but everyone is different. - Kelly

- I went in 2 days before hand to see my office coworkers and just make an appearance. I also started on a Thurs, so I only had to deal with a two day work week. The biggest thing was that I felt so dazed & out of it. I had a lot of problems with concentration and being able to multitask. - Marcia

- I went back one week after the loss of Aiden at 24 weeks. It was too soon so I took another week off after that. I suggest starting back slowly, maybe a half day first. I was lucky to have really supportive co-workers. - Larisa

- I started by going back for a 2 day week. It was helpful to have co-workers visit me at home. It was also suggested that I stop in to the office before starting back. - Jessica

Know that the first day is the worst day.

For many of us, just getting into the building is the hardest obstacle to overcome.

- (Going back to work) was the next step in my healing. It was something I needed to do to start the road back to being me. When I was trying to decide if I should go back to work yet, I realized that if I went back that day or the next week or month the first day would be hard. Take the time that you need only you will know when the time is right. - Kim

- I felt pretty confident driving to work on my first day back. But once I got to the parking lot I started to panic. I called one of my co-workers and she came out to walk in with me. Once I got in the building, it wasn't so bad. - April

- I went back after 2 weeks … However I spent hours just moving piles on my desk because I couldn't focus. – Trisha

Have an escape plan.

Talk with your boss and let them know that you may need to leave early if things become too overwhelming.

- I waited two weeks, and then gave myself permission (and was given official permission) to leave when I had to leave the rest of the month. In fact, I still, 2.5 months later, have really hard days, and just go when I need to. I left this morning after only 20 minutes, in fact, and I don't feel bad about it. Thankfully (so far) my co-workers have been very understanding, although pretty quiet about my loss. - Amy

- I gave myself a three cry limit. I knew that I'd probably cry at work from time to time, but decided that if I cried three times then it was time to go home. I also go outside for a walk if I feel like I'm starting to get overwhelmed. It always helps. - April

- My boss is letting me come and go as I need and that is really helpful. I like to talk about my son so talking with coworkers is helping. It is like free therapy for me. If you go back and realize you can't be there, then ask to take off a little more time. You will know what is best for you. - Hannah

- I think the nicest thing that was done before my return to work was… I sent out an email to all colleges in the office letting them know that I was returning and the date. I thanked them for their support and encouragement. I also indicated in the message that my emotions are still very high, to please be patient with me and outlined my schedule. They were very kind and supportive upon my return. I returned 6 weeks after our son, the most difficult thing was when people called that did not know asked how the new baby was. - Carla

Be prepared for people to say "the wrong thing" or nothing at all.

Some people will inevitably say things that hurt you. But just know that they mean well. Other people will say nothing at all because they don't know what to say. If you work at a large company, some people may not have even heard about what happened.

- One of the (many) hard parts is learning to cope with people saying the wrong things, or saying nothing at all. Sometimes I cannot believe what people say or do. My best way of dealing with it is reminding myself that (most) people mean well, and even if it sounds wrong, at least they are trying. - Anna Lísa

- Be prepared for someone to have missed the news of your loss and ask how your baby is doing. It's a scary thing to face, but I found that those that asked had only the best intentions. After answering the questions though, maybe take a walk or step away for a few minutes to deal with your emotions, if possible. - Nicole

- Hubby took 2 weeks. I took 3 months due to complications after delivery. Take all the time you need. I found people's questions & comments to be the worst part of going back. Some are thoughtless & uncaring…you definitely find out who cares about you & who is sincere. - Michele

- My advise: don't push yourself. Take as much time as you need. Cry when you need to, it's okay… They may not know exactly how to understand or comfort you, so bear with them too. I had to tell myself most of the time they just don't know what to say or do, so I realized that them just being there, in my presence, meant a lot to me. - Natalie

- I only took 2 and a half days. The best thing for me was being very open about everything with my coworkers. They were some of my biggest supporters and I had just started the job 2 weeks before. I found the more I talk about my baby, the better able to cope I was. - Leah

- I expected people to ignore me when I went back. I just didn't expect it to hurt so much when they did. I had several comments made that hurt. I had to try and remember that they just didn't know any better. I wouldn't have known what to say to anyone before I lost Nathan. - Crystal

Surviving the Holidays
http://facesofloss.com/real-advice/surviving-the-holidays

The holiday season can be an especially difficult time for families that have experienced a loss. We hope that the following tips and advice will help you cope and bring back some of the joy to the holidays.

Do what is right for you.
People may have expectations of you during the holiday season, but don't let them pressure you into doing things you are not ready for.

· Do what feels right for you, and don't let people make you feel bad for feeling sad, if that's how you're feeling. If it brings you comfort, do it. - Rebecca

· You have to celebrate/remember your baby in your own way. And the biggest thing is don't let anyone tell you otherwise. … NEVER allow anyone to tell you how you should grieve and remember your angel. Especially if they have never been through it.- Jen

· Do what YOU NEED to do without apology. If you need to skip things, skip things. If it helps send them a babyloss article or blog post that may have the words you need to use but can't find - Martina

· I think you should do whatever you have to do to get through this time. If you want to avoid things (Christmas parties, whatever), by staying home, or distracting yourself like I did, do it. I have heard of some people having Christmas day on a tropical vacation just to do something totally different than they normally would. - Rochelle

· Don't worry about what anyone expects you to do. You need to do only what you feel is right for you. No one else. If that means no decorating or gifts, then so be it. If people don't like it, that is their problem, not yours. - Cristy

· If it's the first year, sometimes the holidays are too unbearable…then do what works for you and your husband even if it means going on a short vacation away from family. My mistake was feeling obligated to be with family instead of taking care of myself. - Patty

· Do what your heart tells you to do, there's no wrong answers. - LaRene

Find a way to honor your baby.

Whether it's a special ornament, a stocking or a donation in honor of your baby, do something special for him/her and include them in your holiday.

· Honor your baby with an ornament or some special time remembering them. - Kirsten

· I did make an ornament to hang on our tree and sent one to my parents. I wanted to acknowledge him even though I knew I couldn't count on how others would. … If you want to celebrate your child by having a candle lighting, hanging an ornament, a stocking, giving them a gift, donating in their name, DO it. Whatever you do will be right. - Rochelle

· My fiance and I are going to make a donation in Kaden's name and then doing something special in memory of him/her. I plan on doing this every year. - Maureen

· Making your own tradition to include your baby helps. We made a stocking to hang with my baby's name on it. We put toys to take to her resting place. - Patty

- Last year was our first Christmas after losing our daughter. We honored her with her own special tree with special ornaments just for her and let her big brother help decorate it. Don't let anyone tell you what you should or shouldn't do or be feeling. Regardless of how long it has been. Everyone grieves differently. For me… Doing little things (like her tree) helps me do something special for ALL of my children on special occasions and all year long. - Lauren

- What helps me is getting a special ornament for Christmas, it can be anything that helps you get through. Having something little like that, that you can see everyday that makes your heart warm. - Audrey

- We hang a stocking for our babies; every year since 1997 and 1998 - Lisa

- It took a couple of years to start to feel comfortable with the holidays. You just need to do what feels right. We have a mini tree that we decorate in his memory and a stocking that we hang. It's our way to remember our special boy. - Corin

- Find ways to honor your baby. We chose to buy gifts for an Angel Tree child. So, even though we couldn't buy gifts for our child, we were able to help another child have a merrier Christmas. - Nicole

Schedule time to grieve and find a safe place to retreat.

If you plan time for grieving in private it will help you to not become overwhelmed when you are around others. It is also helpful to have a place to retreat (an online message board or a call to a friend) for times you do feel overwhelmed.

- Schedule in time for you to grieve, that way it's less overwhelming when you are at a function, but be kind enough to yourself to leave if you find yourself upset. - Mandy

- Find a "safe place" where people understand and it might help keep you from having to search out support at the holiday parties. My place was a bulletin board. Now-a-days, you could even step out whenever you need to and visit your safe place from a smart phone. - Hope

- Allow yourself to feel sad, even during the holidays. Talk about your baby as much as you'd like. - Nicole

Allow yourself to enjoy the season.

Do not feel guilty if you find yourself being happy during the holidays. It's just proof that you are healing.

- … allow yourself to feel happiness or even joy if it happens to come your way-don't feel guilty for being happy or enjoying yourself. Try to live in the moment or "the holiday season" may feel overwhelming. - Rebecca

Kaddish; & what to do when you can't recite it

http://www.jewishpregnancyloss.org/kaddish-what-to-do-when-you-cant-recite-it/

Kaddish

Kaddish is probably the prayer most associated with death and burial, and the recitation of such a familiar formula can be soothing. It can be very hard to be unable to say kaddish on losing a pregnancy, and so it is worthwhile to reflect on the meaning of the prayer, and on alternatives to fill the ritual gap.

What is Kaddish?

The essence of the kaddish prayer is a proclamation of God's unchanging Glory; in contrast to the suffering and pain which shadows our lives, God's grandeur is forever unsullied. It is not, as it is sometimes called, a Jewish prayer for the dead; in fact death is not mentioned in it. There are a number of versions of kaddish, recited at different times, but the shared component to them all is the listeners' response of 'May His great Name be blessed forever and for eternity'. By eliciting this response, the mourner causes all of his/her listeners to publicly acknowledge and beautify God's Name (a kiddush Hashem-sanctification of the Name). The Sages explain that a soul in heaven can no longer follow God's commands to acquire more merit before Him, but that we who remain in this world can do so on behalf of our loved ones. The merit of having created a kiddush Hashem is then credited to the account of the deceased, and considered as though he/she had performed that mitzvah.

We see then that the primary reason for a mourner to recite kaddish is to create a public, articulated recognition of God in the merit of his/her loved one. With this understanding, we can turn to alternative ways of achieving the same effect, at times when saying kaddish is not open to us…

Alternatives to saying kaddish:

1: Bring others closer to God.

Bringing others close to God and Torah is another form of sanctifying His Name; an even better one, perhaps, as you can initiate a deeper realization of God within another Jew. This could be in the form of inviting less-religious friends round for a Shabbat or Festival meal, or to join you in creating the special atmosphere of a Shabbat meal if you don't regularly do so; joining Partners in Torah or Seed to share your knowledge with someone who wants to learn more; or helping in some form or other at any one of the many organizations that bring Jews closer to God

2: Become a living advertisement for the beauty of Judaism.

Unfortunately, we all know the embarrassment of seeing Jews in the newspapers for fraud or other crimes. By conducting our daily interpersonal activities with honesty, integrity, sensitivity and consideration, we have the opposite effect, especially when those watching us know we are Jews. When we behave in an exemplary manner, however small the issue, it creates a sanctification of God's Name. This elevation of all our actions, from the most trivial upwards, can be in merit of your baby.

3. Take on new mitzvot.

Even the smallest extra effort in our relationship with God is valuable, and can be done in memory of your baby. Giving to charity (perhaps one for babies and/or children; it does not need to be a Jewish charity); making an extra step in keeping Shabbat or keeping kosher; taking more care to pray or recite brachos (blessings) clearly; visiting the lonely or sick; providing meals for the hungry - the list is endless, and encompasses wherever your talents lie.

4. Learn Torah, and then say Kaddish at a Siyum.

Kaddish was first written by the Rabbis of the Talmud to be recited at the end of a session of Torah learning. While we no longer recite it each time we finish learning, we preserve this in the existence of a special version of kaddish to be recited at a Siyum.

What is a Siyum?

A siyum – סיום is a celebration of the completion of a significant amount of Torah learning. The word itself means conclusion or finale. Tradition outlines how much one should learn in order to mark it with a siyum, an amount which varies from person to person, depending on how familiar he/she is with Torah texts. Thus for one person, having completed learning a Sedra in Hebrew is a notable achievement, which the next person could only match by completing an entire tractate of Talmud. For help in setting a goal in learning, ask your local rabbi, or one of the many Jewish organizations which will help you to create a learning program and match you up with a learning partner to help you to achieve it.

It is traditional to undertake to learn a set amount of Torah in memory of the departed, to be completed by the sheloshim (the thirtieth day after burial), and/or by the yahrzeit (the yearly anniversary of the Hebrew date of burial). Traditionally, Mishnayot are learned, as the word Mishna המשנה is an anagram of neshama, הנשמה, meaning 'soul', but you can choose any Jewish text. Often more than one person will join in the learning task; for example, friends and family might each learn a tractate of Mishna (or a certain number of chapters, depending on experience), so that between them an 'order', or even the entirety, of Mishna is finished by the end of the sheloshim/yahrzeit. The learning can be done by both men and women, in the baby's memory, so that his/her soul, which had so little time in this world, can enjoy this special commandment.

A siyum requires a minyan of ten adult males, and as with all Jewish events requires a special meal. This is termed a 'seudat mitzva'; a meal of great spiritual merit. It is best for the meal to include bread, or at least cake (in Jewish law, a meal, as opposed to a snack, is defined by the inclusion of bread), but it does not need to be lavish. Nice cake and fruit, or bread with simple dips and salads, are fine. The person (or main person) who has completed the learning will read out the last part of the text he/she has learned, in order to include all those present in the learning experience. He/she will also read the beginning of the next text, to indicate that one is never finished learning Torah; to complete one text is to then begin another. He/she will then recite kaddish, and can have in mind that he/she is reciting kaddish for their baby.

The Siyum as Memorial Service:

The siyum can then be used as an opportunity to remember your baby, and to allow friends and family in to comfort you. You could share some memories of your baby or ideas on the nature of loss; prayers or psalms could be recited; a Torah text dealing with loss could be shared; or all of the above.

For suggestions of prayers, texts and psalms, please see Prayers and Texts
A transliteration of Kaddish and some interesting ideas about saying kaddish can be found within the Bereavement booklet at www.jwn.org.uk. Please note that JPL does not endorse and is not responsible for the suggestions in this booklet.

How the Graveyard Became a Place of Peace
http://www.opentohope.com/how-the-graveyard-became-a-place-of-peace/
Written by Alice Wisler on Friday, October 18, 2013

There's the joke about the cemetery. "How many dead people are in there?" The answer: "All of them." Or, "People are dying to get in there." It brought a smile to my lips the first time a ten-year-old told me. But after my son died, I was wondering why there are so many jokes about death and being dead. "We joke about what we fear," Daniel's pediatric oncologist at UNC-Chapel Hill's Hospital told me.

Well, I don't fear the cemetery anymore. The movies and TV shows, especially around Halloween, like to depict the graveyard as a scary place with ghosts and goblins. For me, the graveyard is a place of peace. My children have named the one where four-year-old Daniel is buried Daniel's Place. On cool autumn mornings I like to take a steaming cup of coffee and blanket and visit Daniel's Place. Beside his marker I have created many poems about longing, laughter, memories, and hope. Beside his marker I have seen life through a misty, but realistic pair of eyes.

On his death date and birth date, we send up colorful helium balloons with attached messages. Often we add stickers of animated characters that he liked. We've eaten sweet slices of watermelon, spit the seeds as he used to, had picnics and played softball - all at the cemetery. For a few years after Daniel's death, his father would go to Daniel's Place every week to reflect while smoking a cigar. The cemetery is a part of our lives now. We've yet to see a goblin.

I travel to other places of rest. In New Bern, North Carolina, we took a trolley tour of the city and one of the stops was the cemetery. The stories of the Union and Confederate soldiers told by our guide were fascinating. But the words on the tombstones of children were what I remember the most. They used to write on the infant graves the exact age of the child who died - "*Jeremy Hawthorne, infant son of Zachary and Millie Hawthorne, nine months, two weeks and three days old.*"

In the nearby town of Hillsborough, my family and I took a walk through The Old Town Cemetery, by the Presbyterian Church. The city has deemed this place, constructed in 1757, a historical site. I'm sure one of the reasons is because fame has been buried here: the body of William Hooper, one of the signers of the Declaration of Independence.

While that impresses me, I am more taken with the engraving on the creamy white tomb of a young woman. Someone chose to inscribe the following thoughtful words and within the whole cemetery there is no sentiment that compares:

Sacred to the memory of Mary Shaw
24 years
March 9, 1840

She needs no formal record of her virtues on this cold marble. They are deeply graven on the tablets of many warm and loving hearts, in which her memory is tenderly and sacredly cherished.

I wonder what kind of friend, parent or spouse this Mary was. Truly many must have loved her, been devoted to her, and agonized over her early death.

Beauty is written within the walls of cemeteries for beauty was lived on this earth. Graveyards are places of remembrances, love and warmth. Cemeteries are not scary... ...unless we fear what others will say about us and place on our stones when we are six feet under - perhaps there lies the anxiety. Will I be remembered lovingly? Will anyone miss me? Will friends and family sacredly cherish who I was to them? What legacy have I left behind?

While no one has been perfect and surely we leave behind those who may not have understood why we did the things we did like own a pit bull or hang our laundry out to dry at 2 a.m., hopefully we aren't so far despised that one would choose to have inscribed on our tomb the words on the grave of Gussie of Ocanto, Wisconsin: *Here lies the body of a girl who died, Nobody mourned and nobody cried. How she lived and how she fared, Nobody knew and nobody cared.*

We all get one chance here on this terrestrial ball. Cemeteries speak of that loudly, yet solemnly. Near Daniel's stone is one of an infant who died only days after he was born. What kind of life did he have? What kind of impact? His epitaph proclaims for all who learn from the words on tombs - in this generation and for those that follow - *"We're so glad you came."* I imagine his parents devastated over the brevity of their son's life and yet, at the same time, delighted to have known him.

I prefer to take my coffee to the cemeteries. I do learn from the dead. Gone are my days of being ruled by fear and trying to laugh the inevitable off. At the cemeteries I learn how I can best live with each day I am given. Now.

Copyright 2002 by Alice J. Wisler

GRANDPARENT GRIEF

http://www.healingheart.net/articles/grandparents_grief.html

by Margaret H. Gerner

I am powerlessness. I am helplessness. I am frustration. I sit with her and I cry with her. She cries for her daughter and I cry for mine. I can't help her. I can't reach inside her and take her broken heart. I must watch her suffer day after day.

I listen to her tell me over and over how she misses Emily, how she wants her back. I can't bring Emily back for her. I can't buy her an even better Emily than she had, like I could buy her an even better toy when she was a child. I can't kiss the hurt and make it go away. I can't even kiss even a small part of it away. There's no bandaid large enough to cover her bleeding heart.

There was a time I could listen to her talk about a fickle boyfriend and tell her it would be okay, and know in my heart that in two weeks she wouldn't even think of him. Can I tell her it'll be okay in two years when I know it will never be okay, that she will carry this pain of "what might have been" in her deepest heart for the rest of her life?

I see this young woman, my child, who was once carefree and fun loving and bubbling with life, slumped in a chair with her eyes full of agony. Where is my power now? Where is my mother's bag of tricks that will make it all better.

Why can't I join her in the aloneness of her grief? As tight as my arms wrap around her, I can't reach that aloneness.

What can I give her to make her better? A cold, wet cloth will ease the swelling of her crying eyes, but it won't stop the reason for her tears. What treat will bring joy back to her? What prize will bring that happy child smile back? Where are the magic words to give her comfort? What chapter in Dr. Spock tells me how to do this? He has told me everything else I've needed to know.

Where are the answers?

I should have them.

I'm the mother.

I know that someday she'll find happiness again, that her life will have meaning again. I can hold out hope for her someday, but what about now? this minute? this hour? this day?

I can give her my love and my prayers and my care and my concern. I could give her my life. But even that won't help.

I wrote this piece out of deep feelings of powerlessness. It seemed that no matter what I did, I could not take away my daughter's pain at the death of her 3 year old daughter, Emily. Were that not enough, I was devastated by my own grief at the loss of my precious granddaughter.

I could relate to my daughter's pain. I, too, had lost a child. In 1971 my six year old son, Arthur, was killed by an automobile. At that time there were no support groups. I didn't know how to grieve or that what I was feeling was normal. I thought I was losing my mind. The psychiatrist I saw after Arthur's death reinforced my belief by giving me drugs for my "depression."

I tried to do what people told me to do; count my blessings and be "strong." That meant not talking about Arthur, not crying, and not expressing any other emotions I felt. The result was five years of distorted, prolonged grief which eventually had to be resolved with the help of a professional who had training in bereavement.

When my daughter lost her child -- that very day in the hospital, with Emily growing cold under my hands -- I swore this would not happen to Dorothy. I didn't know how, but I knew I was going to do everything possible to help her. I knew what she had ahead of her.

I was shattered by Emily's death, but my grief lessened sooner than Dorothy's. Since Emily was not my child, I recovered many months ahead of my daughter. What didn't lessen was seeing Dorothy's pain. That continues, at times, even today.

As a parent of a grieving child, you have a unique opportunity to cement a deep and lasting relationship with your child.
* You have the opportunity to walk with your child through the most difficult life experience they will endure.
* You have the opportunity to help your child in a very special way and the bond that forms will never be broken.

It will not be easy, and the process is long and hard. You will feel powerless, frustrated and helpless many times.

But you CAN help!

Reprinted from Centering Corporation pamphlet For Bereaved Grandparents.

Grief and Intimacy
By Paul C. Rosenblatt, Ph.D.
The Compassionate Friends
We Need Not Walk Alone
Copyright 2002 - 2012

During my interviews with bereaved parents, I've heard most say that the death of a child changes everything. So of course it's not a surprise that many report changes in their sexual relationship after their child dies. These changes might be brief or might last for months, even years. But as with other aspects of the grieving process, it can help couples to know what other bereaved men and women have to say about their experience. Grief has profound effects on a couple. One or both partners may feel fatigued or low in energy. One or both may feel too depressed to care or to have the motivation to do anything, let alone something that requires as much energy as a sexual relationship. Some feel numb in ways that make it impossible to get interested. Some say they feel too fragile, breakable, easily injured, or unconfident.

.. *Rosa: It basically killed sex. That part of our relationship died and it's still not back to where I'd like it to be. Part of it was your grieving. It was really hard to get you excited [laughs] about anything for a long time. And if I pushed or tried to seduce, it made you run away.*

Some parents describe a feeling of "this is how we made our child," that makes intercourse feel inappropriate, uncomfortable, painful, even repulsive.

.. Bruce: We went without contact for months. Even the physical act became frightening and nauseating to *me. It was such a gruesome experience for both of us. I don't recall exactly when we did resume. My guess is probably six, seven months following his death we started having intercourse. But all the time we weren't, we were very much in love, hugging and touching.*

For some, the child's death makes relationships a sacred act, so sacred they hesitate to approach one another.

.. *Glenda: For a long time it was like, That's how we got him. Get away! I couldn't. Remember how I cried? [Ken: Ooh, yeah.] I think more for me it was very painful emotionally for a while. [Ken: Yeah.] It was like, We created him this way; we can't do this.*

Some bereaved parents are afraid they might become pregnant; they feel too vulnerable to risk making and possibly losing another child. Or they feel they have nothing to give; they don't have the necessary energy or the capacity to focus on a baby.

.. *Amy: Even though I knew it was hard to get pregnant, I did not want to get pregnant again right away. There was no way. Whatever birth control we were using at that time, you can't make a mistake. I didn't feel like I needed to [take the risk].*

For a lot of bereaved parents, intercourse seems wrong or strange because it is pleasurable in their grief, pleasure seems wrong, maybe even sinful.

Some grieving parents feel too distant, angry, upset, or frustrated with their partner to want to be intimate: How can I be close with him when he's so unsupportive? When she's not grieving the way I think she should grieve? When he's partly responsible for the death? When . . . ?

In other couples, one or both take an antidepressant that suppresses sexuality. In a few couples, the gap in relations is linked to problems in communication, trust, or mutual respect that were there all along, but were magnified by the death. For those couples, staying together may require competent professional help.

> *Hannah: Things come to the surface that you wouldn't think about, unless something happened. Our marital problems have always been there, but they're more on the surface because of what we've been through. I don't know what's gonna happen. It's kind of a shame to throw away 30 years. The problems that we are having have always [Fred: Yeah.] been there. We just never dealt with them before.*

Living with a Change

From the beginning, or after a while, at least one partner wants to return to something like normal marital relations. Some partners try to seduce their spouse. But seduction doesn't necessarily work. From another perspective, grieving couples have to deal with all sorts of differences, so it's no surprise that they might have to deal with differences in interest in sexuality. One basis for the disparity might be individual preferences in what each finds comforting. For some, maybe men more than women, intercourse is comforting, and in their grief they ache for that comfort.

In couples for whom conceiving a baby is still possible, one partner, usually the woman more than the man, might want to try to become pregnant. But her desire to make a baby or her uncharacteristic sexual aggressiveness may put off her partner, who may then resist her advances.

> *Tina: I think initially we were very close emotionally and sexually. As we moved a little bit further out from it, and then there was talk of being pregnant, it was like he thought the only reason I wanted to have sex was so I could get pregnant. And there was a lot of tension about that, a lot of fights. If he thought that we were gonna be close to being sexual, it was like he'd do everything in his power not to do anything. I remember, goin' through my mind, "That's it! We're done! I'm divorced! I'm leavin' him!"*

Expressing Closeness

For some bereaved couples, touching, hugging, and cuddling continue. They can feel loved and the comfort of skin-to-skin contact without going further. In fact, many people think of touching, hugging, and cuddling, as sexual, so not having intercourse doesn't mean they stop being sexual. However, just as couples may experience a decline or a gap in relations, they may experience a decline in touching, hugging, and cuddling.

> *Brett: There were a lot of things I needed, but I didn't get from her. And there was a lotta, just even the hugging, the holding, even some talking about it. And it wasn't her job to fix me. There wasn't anybody that was capable of doing that.*
> *Joan: I think there would've been times even when he wanted to hug me or he wanted to give me support, and I just didn't want it. I just felt like I wanted to deal with my grief myself.*
> *Brett: That was so uncharacteristic, that you weren't there.*

Brett and Joan eventually returned to being fully in contact, and that was the experience of most other couples who talked with me about a gap or decline in touching, hugging, and cuddling.

New Emotions

For couples who continue to have marital relations after a child dies, and for those who return after a gap, the experience is often different in important ways from what it was before the child died. What is most commonly reported is that relations are emotionally charged and immensely meaningful in new ways. For many bereaved parents, sex becomes, at least when first resumed, a powerful, life-affirming experience, a symbol of healing and being back together as a couple. For many bereaved parents, the act has new meanings that bring up powerful new emotions. The emotions may be felt or expressed in different ways, but it is common for tears to be part of it all.

- *Joy: I can't even remember the first time that we made love after the accident, but I remember always just really crying after it, just sobbing, and just bringing so many emotions to the surface, and I used to think, "Aw, he's going to quit making love to me 'cause all I do is sob afterwards'."*

- *Jane: One thing I've noticed, any time we were intimate, almost always, even though I wasn't sobbing or anything like this, just the emotion. Almost every time one or the other of us would say, and it just really didn't exactly relate, and yet we just really missed him. You just were emotional, and that was the biggest emotion in our lives. We just missed him and so frequently I would get tears in my eyes, or my husband would, and we would just say to each other, "I sure still miss him."*

Patience

For bereaved parents, it may be helpful to know that our research indicates that a break or decline in a couple's sexual relationship or in touching, hugging, and cuddling is not so much a difficulty as one of the things that often happens when a child dies. It's not a sign of anything disastrous in the couple's relationship or a warning about future difficulties. As with other aspects of the grief process, declines or gaps in physical contact call for patience and understanding. In the long run, many couples move on to profound depths of intimacy and develop greater mutual understanding, empathy, and communication through the process of grieving and loving together.

(Bio dated 2002) Paul Rosenblatt is the Morse Alumni Distinguished Teaching Professor of Family Social Science at the University of Minnesota. His research interests have long focused the impact of grief on the family. His grandson, Eli Rosenblatt, died at age two in 1990. Paul is the founder of the Grief and Families Focus Group of the National Council on Family Relations and the author of several books including "Help Your Marriage Survive the Death of a Child" and dozens of scholarly articles.

Reconciling Grief: Take All the Time You Need
Written by Harriet Hodgson on Friday, August 21, 2009
http://www.opentohope.com/reconciling-grief-take-all-the-time-you-need/

Mourners want grief to end. Some try to rush their mourning, only to find it cannot be rushed. According to The Talmud, "Who forces time is pushed back by time; who yields to time finds time is on his side." The process of reconciliation - making the deceased part of yourself and your life - is a slow one. It's even slower if you have suffered multiple losses.

Colin Murray Parkes writes about time in "All in the End is Harvest." He says, "Death may happen in a moment, but grief takes time; and that time is both an ordeal and a blessing." Grief work is also an ordeal and a blessing and you must do it in order to recover from loss and move forward with life.

Taking your time helps you do your grief work. What is grief work? The National Cancer Institute defines it as the "processes that a mourner needs to complete before resuming daily life." Grief work is a lonely work and nobody can do it for you. When you take your journal entries, counseling, support group meetings, creating art work, and memorials.

Taking your time helps you to sort feelings. Grief causes conflicting emotions. You may have a sense of relief if your loved one was in hospice and you have been expecting his or her death. On the other hand, you may be angry at God and ask, "Why did this happen to me?" Kevin Hendry examines feelings in a Forbes Health Foundation article, "Guidelines for Doing Good Grief Work." Mourners should honor their feelings, Hendry says, for "your healing will be found at the heart of the whole huge unspeakably intense and disorderly jumble of them all."

Taking your time increases self-awareness. Daniel Goleman, PhD, discusses self-awareness in his book, "Emotional Intelligence: Why it Can Matter More Than IQ." According to Goleman, self-awareness is "ongoing attention to one's internal states." Goldman says self-awareness doesn't get carried away by emotions, but is present "even amidst turbulent emotions." This is good news for mourners. Despite the pain you are feeling, you may be self-aware and listen to our inner voice.

Taking your time helps you to let go. The Coping Website, a public service of James J. Messina, PhD and Constance M. Messina, PhD, lists the tools for letting go. The authors think letting go is "a decision to take action that will result in a significant change in your life." In order to move forward with life you have to let go of many things: cause of death, memories, feelings, possessions, events, and more. Letting go will lift your spirits.

Coming to terms with grief takes time, according to a Grief Watch Website article, "Normal Reactions to Loss: The Mourning Process." It's hard to believe now, the day will come when you are aware of the progress you have made and have hope for the future. "You will be different," the article notes, "and a 'healed scar' will be where the rawness once was." So take the time you need - minutes, hours, days - to reconcile your grief and create a new life.

Copyright 2009 by Harriet Hodgson

Harriet Hodgson, BS, MA, has been an independent journalist for 30 years. She is a member of the American Society of Journalists and Authors, the Association of Health Care Journalists and the Association for Death Education and Counseling.

Responding to Children's Questions about Death
by Linda Goldman

Published in Fall 2009 Bereavement Publications, Inc. Living With Loss™ Magazine
Excerpts from Great Answers to Difficult Questions about Death: What Children Need to Know. Linda Goldman, Jessica Kingsley Publishers 2009

Children's questions are a window to their soul - and a mirror
to their inner thoughts and feelings.

Death is a difficult topic

Death is a difficult and sensitive topic to discuss with children. So often adults feel at a loss for words. Without knowing what to say or how to say it, many parents and professionals avoid children's questions. Some refuse to respond at all. Eight-year-old Alice explained a disturbing event. She told her teacher about her dad's death during the very first week of school. Her teacher never said a word. Infuriated and saddened, Alice asked over and over, "Why didn't my teacher ever say anything back?"

Often girls and boys share how angry and alone they feel at being dismissed or ignored when asking questions about the death of a loved one. "Where did my Mom go?" "Why did Dad have to die?" "Did my doggy suffer?" "Will I die too?" are very common thoughts for girls and boys to have.

Responding with care can normalize children's uncomfortable ideas and feelings. Acknowledging their questions is a valuable tool to reassure them and help them feel safe.

Honoring children's questions

We may feel terrified when confronted by a child with a question about death, and send a conscious or unconscious message inhibiting further discussion. When adults respond to questions in ways that are more complicated than necessary, children can become overwhelmed. When adults limit replies or refuse to answer - kids get the message. Death is a closed topic - don't ask again.

Joey's mom wanted to know "What do I do when my-five-year-old asks so many questions about death?" One health care professional responded to Joey's mother in this way. "My daughter Emily is five. She also asked too many questions about death. I explained to her she could only ask two questions a day. If she asked more than that she would need to go to her room for a half hour and think about it. This really worked. Within one month's time Emily never asked another question about death." Emily got the message in no uncertain terms - stop asking about death.

Placing restrictions or discounting children's questions will work to extinguish asking them. Our goal is to create an environment where all questions are welcomed, accepted, and responded to openly and without judgment. The purpose of this book is to share simple and direct dialogues about death to facilitate open communication. Comfortable language is a useful instrument for all caring adults to share appropriate responses that are satisfying to young people.

Developmental understandings

Children re-grieve at different developmental stages. During early childhood they are usually satisfied with a simple definition and explanation. They see death as reversible and have egocentric ideas involving magical thinking. Many times they believe they caused their person's death.

As they get older they become more curious about the facts of the death, and may come back at ages 8, 9, and 10 and re-visit the death with new interest and inquisitiveness. In pre-adolescence and adolescence they approach their strong need to look to their own age group to find answers.

At this age girls and boys begin to see death is not reversible. Life is finite. Young people begin to form their own spiritual belief system and look to their peers for support and understanding. They feel empowered to become advocates for causes related to their person's death.

Responding to a Question

Children need to be told the truth about a death in an age appropriate way. They usually know when they are being lied to. So often lies create a secondary loss of the trust of their emotional environment.

There are many ways people die. Often adults have difficulty in finding the precise words to use to explain a fatal Illness, sudden accident, murders, suicide, or natural or man-made catastrophe. They are surprised when many girls and boys are satisfied with simple and honest responses appropriate to their developmental stage. Six-year-old Rebecca asked, "How did mommy die?" "She got very sick." might be just enough of a response.

Greg (5): A Case Study

Five-year-old Greg was sad. His pet gerbil, Jasper, had died. Jasper was lying in the cage very still. Greg started screaming and crying and Mom ran into the room to see what happened. "Something is wrong with Jasper. He isn't moving. I'm scared." Mom had a tear in her eye. "Jasper died sweetie." Greg put his hands over his ears. "No! No! That can't be true."

What does dead mean?

Death means when the body stops working. Sometimes people die when they are very, very, very old, or very, very, very sick, or they are so, so, so injured that the doctors and nurses can't make their bodies work any more. Jasper is dead. It is sad. He will not move, not be warm, and not be alive again.

What can't you do when your body doesn't work?

You can't eat, you can't play, you can't watch TV - you can't even breathe. Jasper has died. His body is getting cold. It stopped working and he can't even run in his cage.

But where does his body go?

Animals and people can be buried in the ground. When you are ready, we can find a box to bury Jasper in. We can put a soft blanket inside with Jasper's body and you can put in some-thing special too.

Can I put in a picture of me?

He would like that. Then he won't feel so alone. Let's put his toy in too.

That sounds like a great idea. We can decorate the box with things that remind you of Jasper.

Can we bury Jasper together?

Yes, it is nice to have a ceremony where everyone can do something. You could say a prayer, light a candle, send off a balloon, or plant a flower. It feels good to do something special after a death.

Concluding thought

Telling children the truth in age appropriate ways is helpful in securing their trust. In order to communicate we need clear and simple language for dialogues. Preparing answers and dialogues using definitions of death and of specific ways people die can encourage open communication and maintain a level of acceptance for the grieving child.

Suggested Books

Grief

· They Were Still Born: Personal Stories About Stillbirth - Janel C. Atlas, Ed.

· An Exact Replica of a Figment of My Imagination - Elizabeth McCracken

· Empty Cradle, Broken Heart: Surviving the Death of Your Baby - Deborah L. Davis

· Three Minus One: Stories of Parents' Love and Loss - Kelly Kittel

· Tear Soup: A Recipe for Healing After Loss - Pat Schweibert, Chuck DeKlye

· When Hello Means Goodbye: A Guide for Parents Whose Child Dies Before Birth, at Birth, or Shortly After Birth - Pat Schweibert, Paul Kirk

· A Guide for Fathers When a Baby Dies - Tim Nelson

· Empty Arms: Hope and Support for Those Who Have Suffered a Miscarriage, Stillbirth or Tubal Pregnancy - Pam Vredevelt

Medical Termination of a Pregnancy

· Knocked Up, Knocked Down: Postcards of Miscarriage and Other Misadventures From the Brink of Parenthood - Monica Murphy Lemoine

· Our Heartbreaking Choices: 46 Women Share Their Stories of Interrupting a Much-Wanted Pregnancy - Christie Brooks

Pregnancy After a Loss

· Journeys: Stories of Pregnancy After Loss - Amy Abbey, Ed.

· Trying Again - A Guide to Pregnancy After Miscarriage, Stillbirth, and Infant Loss - Ann Douglass and John R. Sussman

· Pregnancy After a Loss: A Guide to Pregnancy After a Miscarriage, Stillbirth, or Infant Death – Carol Cirulli Lanham

Infertility

· Pregnant With Hope: Good News for Infertile Couples - Susan Radulovacki

· Dear God, Why Can't I Have a Baby: A Companion Guide for Couples on the Infertility Journey - Janet Thompson

· Empty Womb, Aching Heart: Hope and Help for Those Struggling with Infertility - Marlo Schalesky

Blogs and Websites

Websites
- Facesofloss.com
- Opentohope.com
- Stillstandingmag.com
- Bereavedparentsusa.org - Support for the loss of a child, grandchild, or sibling
- Climbsupport.org - Support for the death of one or more children in a set of multiples
- Healingheart.net - Support for grandparents
- Firstcandle.org - Bilingual support
- Aheartbreakingchoice.com - For parents whose child has life-limiting conditions
- GriefWatch.com
- Compassionatefriends.org
- Griefnet.org – Online support group

Blogs
- Infantangel.wordpress.com
- Amourningmom.com
- Rememberingporter.com
- Littlegreenfamily.com
- Missinggrace.com
- Littlewingedones.wordpress.com
- Mommadale.wordpress.com
- Fathersgrievinginfantloss.com

National and International Nonprofit Organizations

- Pregnancy Loss and Infant Death Alliance (PLIDA) – Provides education and awareness around the needs of bereaved families
- First Candle / SIDS Alliance – A research / advocacy group on stillbirth, miscarriage and Sudden Infant Death Syndrome
- The Star Legacy Foundation for Stillbirth Awareness – Raises funding and awareness to support stillbirth research and education

AFTERWORD

The loss of a baby is heart-wrenching, gut-wrenching.

The loss of a baby is life-changing.

Keep this book close.   The bloggers and authors represented here, as well as the websites and support groups listed, will continue to offer support and guidance as you continue in your search for healing.   Find a support group so you can speak with people who truly understand this thing that has happened to you.

Remember, you will never forget this – it will never go away.   Twenty years from now you will still sorrow, but your sorrow will have a different feel than it does now.   Do your best to walk through the storm – to the path of healing.

We know you can make it.

When you walk through a storm

Hold your head up high

And don't be afraid of the dark.

At the end of the storm

Is a golden sky….

You'll Never Walk Alone

Carousel

Oscar Hammerstein/Richard Rodgers

ABOUT THE AUTHOR

Karen Shipp earned a Bachelor of Science degree in Nursing in 1977. For the next 33 years she had the honor of participating in the birth experience of thousands of families. Along the way she earned a Master of Science degree in Community Counseling and incorporated those skills into supporting the psychological experience of childbirth. In 2012 she retired from the physical demands of one of the country's largest Labor & Delivery units to concentrate on other aspects of the birth experience beyond those encountered in the hospital setting. Since that time she has worked with the Perinatal Bereavement Office at Northside Hospital in Atlanta, GA, as a volunteer and has seen first-hand the long-term psychological struggles of families who have lost or are anticipating the loss of their baby.

She is currently pursuing writing opportunities to share her knowledge and experience in Maternal and Child Health to benefit those families who represent the lifeblood of her career. She is a member of the Association of Women's Health, Obstetric, and Neonatal Nursing, and the Pregnancy Loss and Infant Death Alliance (PLIDA). She is currently pursuing Certification in Grief Counseling from the American Institute of Health Care Professionals, Inc., and the American Academy of Grief Counseling.

Made in the USA
Columbia, SC
19 February 2022

56469974R00053